Awakening to the Noble Truth

Curriculum

Prayers,

Khenpo Lama Migmar Tseten

Mangalamkosha Publications
PO Box 391042
Cambridge, MA 02139 USA
www.lamamigmar.net

ISBN 978-1532869167

Preface

The following curriculum is a step by step study guide to assist students in contemplating the Four Noble Truths. This companion volume delves further into the content of our publication "Awakening to the Noble Truth." The Four Noble Truths are regarded as the central teaching of the Buddhist tradition and provide the framework upon which all other Buddhist philosophy and meditation are based. These Noble Truths are: the truth of suffering, the origin of suffering, the cessation of suffering, and the noble Eightfold path leading to nirvāṇa.

Although we may already be familiar with this core doctrine, by repeatedly studying the Four Noble Truths and their sixteen corresponding aspects, our realizations on the spiritual path can become more transformative and profound.

Mangalamkosha Publications
Cambridge, MA
February 2017

Acknowledgements

Mangalamkosha wishes to thank the following people who have helped to bring this curriculum to completion: David Magone, Rev. Judith Wright, Dr. Lucy Phillips, Dr. Raga Markely, Dr. Diana McPhee, Janet Hutchinson and Meg Hutchinson.

Table of Contents

Class One

Introduction to the Four Noble Truths

Objectives

Students will:

- Receive an introduction to the lineage and to Khenpo Migmar Tseten

- Learn about the Buddha Shakyamuni

- Explore a general introduction to the philosophy of the Four Noble Truths

- Explore the three aspects of the first Noble Truth of Suffering: impermanence, suffering, and insubstantiality

- Understand some of the ways in which impermanence creates suffering in our lives

- Learn the three major types of suffering: the suffering of suffering, suffering of change, and the suffering of conditioned nature

- Receive a brief introduction to the five aggregates: form, feeling, ideation, formation and mind/mental consciousness

Class Outline

Introduction:

5 minutes: Begin with a short 5 minute Shamatha meditation.

Lecture

60 minutes

Introduction to the lineage and the program, the Buddha Shakyamuni, and the first, second and third aspects of the First Noble Truth: impermanence, three types of suffering, and insubstantiality. Introduction to the five aggregates.

Q & A

10 minutes: Lead the class through a short Q & A session.

Lecture on the following points:

Teacher introduction

Teacher introduces himself or herself to the students

Lineage introduction

Teacher gives a brief overview of Khenpo Migmar:

- Previous head of the Sakya Center (Rajpur, Dehradun, India) and Sakya Monastery (Puruwalla, India)
- Studied with Khenchen Rinchen Sangpo who was a private tutor to many lineage masters
- Currently serves as Harvard University Buddhist Chaplain

Introduction to the program

- This program will cover a general introduction to the Buddha's teachings on the Four Noble Truths.

The Four Noble Truths:

- Outline the essence of Buddhist practice.
- Provide practical instructions that lead to the cessation of all suffering.

The Four Noble Truths are:

- The truth of suffering
- The truth of the origin of suffering
- The truth of the cessation of the suffering
- The truth of the path leading to the cessation of suffering

Benefits of the Four Noble Truths:

- Instruct us in the right way to live
- Show us how to go beyond suffering
- Lead us toward Enlightenment

Each lesson will delve into a separate aspect of the Four Noble Truths and will include:

- Seated meditation
- Lecture
- Q and A sessions

If you wish to read more about the topics covered in this course, the following books are recommended:

- Awakening to the Noble Truth – Lama Migmar Tseten

- The Wisdom Gone Beyond – Lama Migmar Tseten
- The Abhidharmakosabasyam – Vasubandhu

A Brief History of the Buddha Shakyamuni

Prince Siddhartha

- Nepalese-Indian
- Lived a life of luxury
- Exposed to suffering when he traveled outside the palace
- Realized that no one can avoid the suffering of sickness, old age and death

Siddhartha sees the meditator

In one of his travels outside the palace, Siddhartha saw a meditator and was exposed to the idea of a spiritual life.

- Abandoned life as a prince
- Eventually achieved enlightenment
- Through this realization he came to recognize the Four Noble Truths which include the Noble Eightfold Path

Each of the Four Noble Truths has four different aspects

- Understanding of these aspects is based on our insight and on the clarity of each of our minds.
- As our vision grows purer, these aspects become more apparent.

First three aspects of the first Noble Truth: Impermanence, Suffering and Insubstantiality

The first aspect of the First Noble Truth is the aspect of impermanence.

- Impermanence is the understanding that whatever is created due to causes and conditions is subject to decay.
- Everything is changing, and nothing can remain forever.

In order to understand our own impermanence, we must first examine what we are made of.

- The "five aggregates" are the foundation of our current experience.

The five aggregates are:

- 1.) Form (the physical body and matter)
- 2.) Feelings
- 3.) Ideations
- 4.) Formations (which includes all of the other emotions)
- 5.) Consciousness (the mind and mental consciousness)

We possess a very strong attachment to the five aggregates.

- There is a real conflict between our attachment to these five aggregates and the truth of impermanence.
- We know that we are constantly changing.
- We will eventually grow old and die.

- Due to our very strong attachment to our bodies, we remain in denial about our own impermanence.

All of these aggregates are impermanent and they are continuously in a state of flux.

- Our feelings are changing.
- Our ideas are changing.
- Our emotional states are changing.
- Our consciousness is constantly shifting.

The truth of impermanence and change versus our attachment to the five aggregates creates an underlying conflict in our lives.

- As a consequence, whenever we are confronted with the truth of impermanence we experience tremendous pain and suffering.

The second aspect of the First Noble Truth: Suffering itself. There are three main types of suffering

- The suffering of suffering
- The suffering of change
- The suffering of conditioned nature

The suffering of suffering

- Includes all physical illnesses and discomforts

- Sickness is called the suffering of suffering because it is adding physical or emotional pain to our underlying state of suffering.

The suffering of change

- This suffering actually stems from all of our pleasurable experiences and all of our conditional states of happiness.

- **Example 1**: When you fall in love with someone, you expect that blissful state of happiness to be permanent. When the relationship begins to change, when you begin to see your partner's flaws and you start to argue, you experience much suffering.

- **Example 2**: When you first have a child you are so excited and you feel that your baby is lovely and has made your life complete. Then when the child gets older and begins to separate from you and becomes a difficult teenager, the child can become a source of pain.

Nothing in this life can stay the same but we often remain ignorant of this impermanence.

- What we fail to see is that our suffering is actually rooted in that original happiness.

- All delightful experiences are actually the suffering of change because they become the causes and conditions for future pain and suffering.
- Since anything good will inevitably change, then our greatest pleasure is already sowing the seeds of loss and disappointment.

The Suffering of Conditioned Nature

This third form of suffering is actually the basis for both the suffering of suffering and the suffering of change.

- The suffering of conditioned nature is referring to conception and to the very beginning of the five aggregates within a person.
- You could say that from the very moment that we are conceived we are already beginning to die.
- Everything in this life is conditioned and this impermanence is at the root of all our suffering.

These three kinds of suffering become much more intensified when our emotions are involved.

- The suffering of suffering is related to the destructive emotion of anger.
- The suffering of change is related to emotions of desire and attachment.
- The suffering of conditioned nature is based on our ignorance.

The third aspect of the First Noble Truth: Insubstantiality

- Another way for us to understand the truth of suffering is for us to integrate it into our five aggregates.
- As we have discussed, each person has the five aggregates of form, feeling, ideation, formation, and consciousness.
- Through developing stronger insight meditation we come to know the characteristics of all of these aggregates.

The Aggregate of Form

- By nature, all physical matter is composed of material atoms.
- These atoms are comprised of the four basic elements of earth, water, fire, and air.

If we look deeper into these atoms, then all material things begin to lose their identification.

- At the atomic level, what reference do we have with which to identify an object?
- At the level of the atom we discover the insubstantiality of all objects.

Generally in our lives, we don't break things down to the atomic level.

- Instead we assign an identity or label to each object in the material world.
- Then, based on its usefulness to us, we get attached.

- It is one thing to enjoy something and to let it go, but if we get emotionally attached to it and then something happens to that object, we will experience so much suffering of change.

The first aggregate of "form" or "matter" is what our material body consists of.

- Once we know the nature of our physical bodies, we will also understand the nature of other people's bodies.

In the Sūtras, Buddha said that as our insight meditation deepens, not only do we see impermanence in ourselves, but we can begin to see impermanence in all living beings as well.

- This observation will help us to understand how all other material things outside of our bodies are also impermanent.

This realization also helps us see impermanence in all material things.

- By realizing the changing nature of our own bodies, we can learn to recognize this impermanence in all sentient beings and all physical matter.

The Aggregate of Feeling
The second aggregate is feeling.

- Based on the recognition of our own feelings, we can comprehend that other beings have feelings.

If we look closely at feelings, whether they are pleasure or pain, happiness or unhappiness, even neutral feelings, we see that all feelings are a form of suffering.

- This is because feelings are based on the five aggregates, and the five aggregates are defiled.

By learning to view even our happy feelings as a cause of suffering we can:

- Counteract the misconception that life should always be pleasurable. As long as we are expecting life to be pleasurable, we will constantly be disappointed and experience pain instead.

Even a neutral feeling is a form of suffering.

- Neutral feelings are a result of our underlying ignorance.
- This ignorance is the basis of all the suffering of suffering and the suffering of change.

Through contemplation we can recognize the insubstantiality of feelings.

- If we look closely, can we find any lasting feeling? Any substantial or permanent feeling state?

The same principles apply to the rest of the five aggregates, of Ideation, Formation, and Consciousness respectively.

- They are all insubstantial.
- Insubstantiality is not limited only to material objects.

Consciousness and emotions are not material.

- What is the mind?
- Even with strong insight, if we look into the mind, we cannot actually find the mind!
- The mind loses its own identification.

Q & A

10 minutes: Lead the class through a short Q & A session.

Questions for Review:

- How might you personally benefit from learning about the Four Noble Truths?
- Why do you think that the Buddha emphasized the truth of impermanence first?
- Do you think that an acceptance of impermanence can lead to less suffering? If so, how?
- What are the three different types of suffering that we encounter in life?

- What role does emotion play in the degree to which we suffer?

- Why do you think that the suffering of suffering is related to the destructive emotion of anger?
- How does the suffering of change relate to desire and attachment?
- Why do you think that the suffering of conditioned nature is based on our ignorance?
- How would you describe insubstantiality?

Class Two

The Fourth Aspect of the First Noble Truth: Emptiness

Objectives

Students will:

- Be introduced to the fourth aspect of the First Noble Truth: Emptiness
- Learn how an insight into emptiness can help counter attachment
- Learn how an understanding of emptiness can help us come to grips with our own mortality
- Learn the definition of a "Noble Truth"

Class Outline

Introduction

5 minutes: Begin with a short 5 minute Shamatha meditation.

Lecture

60 minutes: The fourth aspect of the First Noble Truth: Emptiness.

Q & A

10 minutes: Lead the class through a short Q & A session.

Lecture on the following points:

The fourth aspect of the First Noble Truth is emptiness.
- When we look deeper and deeper into any of the five aggregates, we cannot find lasting evidence of them.
- As our meditation deepens, we begin to go beyond all concepts, beyond all identification of objects, to discover the emptiness-nature.

Right now in our lives, we have lots of attachment to objects.
- Whenever something happens to those objects of attachment we experience pain and suffering.
- This is due to the fact that we have believed that these objects are real and substantial.

It is very difficult for us to see the emptiness-nature without meditation experience.
- An understanding of impermanence can only arise from deep insight meditation experience.
- Through meditative reflection, we see the impermanent and empty nature of all things.

This realization counteracts our misconceptions of reality.

- As long as we have emotional attachment to objects, thinking that they are real, we will experience much pain and sadness when we lose them.

To counteract these attachments, we need to develop a profound understanding of emptiness.

- We need to reflect on the emptiness of those objects, emotions, thoughts, and even of the mind itself.

Reflecting and meditating on each aspect of the Four Noble Truths helps to counteract all our misconceptions about reality. Understanding emptiness can help us come to terms with our own mortality.

- In our lives we cling to the idea of a "self."
- Most of what we do in our lives is based on "self-cherishing" because we believe that the self and ego truly exist.

As we have discussed, the objects of all of our attachments are rooted in the five aggregates.

- This self-cherishing is based on attachment to our bodies, our feelings, our ideas, our formations/habitual patterns, and our consciousness.
- When we look deeper, we discover there is no substance to what we thought was existing.

Emptiness, the fourth aspect of the First Noble Truth, includes not only the emptiness-nature of ourselves, but of other objects as well.

- They are all empty.
- The insubstantiality and emptiness aspects help us to overcome the misconception of self, which is based on our five aggregates.

These aspects also help us to overcome all our ideas of ownership based on our sense of self.

- Concepts like "my" are based on the idea of the phenomenal self arising from the five aggregates.
- These notions of "my house" or "my car" are all arising from misconceptions related to the five aggregates.

We each have attachment to ourselves and to the whole universe.

- It is very important to understand the aspects of insubstantiality and emptiness in order to counteract these attachments.

We can study the Four Noble Truths and gain some intellectual understanding.

- This intellectual understanding will only become a "Noble Truth" when we realize this experience through deep insight meditation.

Through meditation we learn to see these four aspects: Impermanence, Suffering, Insubstantiality, and Emptiness.

We learn to see these aspects in all five aggregates of ourselves, other beings, and all other things in the conditioned world.

- When we see in this way, then we are seeing the First Noble Truth because we are seeing right through our misconceptions.
- We are no longer clouded by our desires. We are no longer seeing reality through anger or ignorance.

At this level, we have gone beyond all three afflictive emotions of attachment, anger, and ignorance.

- We have stopped viewing the world through the lens of these emotions.
- We have stopped relating to ourselves and those around us with desire, anger, or indifference.
- As a result, we are gaining some wisdom, some equanimity in our experience.

The Noble Truth or insight means seeing with wisdom— seeing with an equanimity that is free from all destructive emotions.

- We no longer have the inner conditions with which we falsely project our emotions onto an object.

- Because of this, the way we see reality will be very different.

That's why it is called a "Noble Truth."

- When we see beyond our delusions, we will realize for the first time that what we saw before was actually defiled.
- We will realize that our old way of seeing was tainted because it was all based on misconceptions.

The way yogis see, and the way we see now, are two completely different experiences of reality!

- What we see is based on ignoble perceptions.
- If we have ignorance, then we will have all the other emotions.
- Everything we see will be affected by those other emotions.

But when we can see through our delusions to the Noble Truth, we recognize that the nature of all our feelings was suffering.

- Only nirvāṇa is unconditioned and is beyond death.
- Nirvāṇa is the cessation of feelings that were rooted in the ego.

All feelings, even neutral feelings, are rooted in the ego.

- The seed of these feelings is poisonous. Whatever grows from such a seed is always poisonous.

- But through practice, as we recognize the wisdom of the Four Noble Truths, we will see that there is an entirely new way to experience our lives.

Q & A

15 - 20 minutes: Lead the class through a short Q & A session.

Questions for Review:

- How would you describe the term "emptiness" in your own words?
- Does relating to people, concepts and things as "inherently real" create obstacles to peace and understanding? If so, in what ways?
- In what ways does developing deeper insights into emptiness help to counteract suffering?
- Why are the Noble Truths referred to as noble?
- Is there any state beyond death and suffering? If so, what is it's name?

Class Three

Intro to the Second Noble Truth: Cause and Origination

Objectives

Students will:

- Formulate a basic understanding of Karma
- Learn that everything has a cause, condition, and result
- Discover some of the ways in which Karma creates suffering
- Learn how the second aspect of the second Noble Truth "origination" negates the idea of a first or singular cause

Class Outline

Introduction

5 minutes: Begin with a short 5 minute Shamatha meditation.

Lecture

60 minutes

Introduce the Second Noble Truth: The Origin of Suffering. Give an overview of the First and Second Aspects of the Second Noble Truth: Cause and Origination.

Q & A

10 minutes

Lecture on the following points:

The Second Noble Truth is the Origin of Suffering.

- As we have established in the First Noble Truth, the nature of conditioned existence is suffering.
- The Second Noble Truth looks closely at the origins of that suffering.

Origination is more subtle because we often don't see origination directly.

- Buddha taught four different aspects related to the Second Noble Truth.
- These aspects help to clear away our misconceptions related to the origin of suffering.

The first aspect of the Second Noble Truth is Cause.

- This is to help us see the true source of our pain and suffering.

If we look closely, we can see that pretty much all suffering has some cause.

- The causes are complex and subtle.

- There are different durations of time we experience these sufferings.
- Sometimes we cannot remember the causes of our suffering because the suffering has extended over many lifetimes.

Example: When we experience the suffering of suffering in the form of a headache, we feel the pain of that headache, but we might not know what the real causes are.

- There can be many different kinds of headaches: there are migraine headaches and stress headaches.
- Some headaches are a warning sign of a stroke.
- We feel the pain, but the cause can be many different things.

In these cases it can be helpful to go to a doctor for diagnosis.

- We may go to the doctor and receive many different tests.
- Sometimes a doctor can offer a solution.

With Karma, the diagnosis can be challenging because Karma is complex.

- There are many reasons why our attempts to determine the causes of suffering can lead to misunderstanding.
- There are many schools of thought.

Perhaps the reason why Buddha taught cause as the first aspect of the Second Noble Truth is because there are many people who don't accept the natural law of karma.

- Doctors don't necessarily accept karma.
- From a medical standpoint, doctors may determine the causes for a physical illness and accept that as the original cause of that particular suffering.
- If they find an obvious physical explanation for a particular illness, they may see that as the only cause
- As a result, they might rarely look deeper at karmic causes and conditions.

The majority of people in the world don't accept karma.

- Many people only accept what they can prove or diagnose materially.
- If something is immaterial, how can they find a diagnosis?

The purpose of the first aspect of the Second Noble Truth is to emphasize the natural law of karma.

What is the law of karma?

- Karma refers to cause, condition, and result.
- Within these three, the natural law of cause and effect also has the meaning of relativity and interdependency.

Many people may not comprehend the depth of karma.

- One reason for this first aspect of "cause" is to prove that everything is interdependent, based on cause, condition, and result.

All three kinds of suffering that we have outlined in the First Noble Truth are interdependent.

- They all have causes and conditions.
- In order to prove this fact, Buddha taught this aspect of Cause.

We can study all the details of different causes, conditions, and results in the Abhidharma.

- Abhidharma is actually the most detailed study of the Four Noble Truths.
- Through extensive study of all of the causes, conditions, and results, we can prove that everything we experience is due to karma.
- We come to understand that experiencing suffering is the result of negative karma.

In fact, everything we experience is due to the interdependency of cause, condition, and result.

- The first aspect of the Second Noble Truth teaches that everything has a cause, condition, and result.
- Each particular cause will have its own particular result.

Example: If we expect a mango seed to grow into a pomegranate, it will never happen!

- The result has to have its own cause and condition.

This is how we can prove that all suffering is caused by negative karma based on negative emotions.

- This demonstrates that all karma is based on specific causes and conditions.
- The negative emotions are the seeds; the suffering is the result.

Once we understand this, we can study the various factors of negative karma.

- We can study the ten negative karmas which correspond to physical, verbal, and mental negative emotions.
- Through the aspect of Cause, we can also study karma in general.
- We can study the causes and results of negative karma.
- The aspect of Cause can prove that everything manifests as a result of this cycle of cause, condition and result.

The second aspect of the Second Noble Truth is "origination."

- Origination here doesn't mean that karma has an origin or a first cause.
- Once we've established interdependency and relativity

between cause, condition, and result, then within interdependency we cannot find a first cause.

Origination in this context is actually referring to that cycle where every cause has its own cause, and that cycle keeps repeating again and again.

- Each past cause and condition has a present result.
- The present result is the cause and condition for a future result.
- This is the cycle through which everything originates.

We could also say that origination proves that there is no first cause and also no singular cause.

- Take for example how one entity can be both cause and result.
- **Example:** One man can be a son to his own father and also a father to his own son simultaneously.
- He's one person, but he can be referred to in multiple ways.

In "dependent origination," causes are always multiple.

- They are multiple in the sense that one entity can have different aspects.
- The entity can be a result, a cause, or a condition, depending on our frame of reference.
- That's why the second aspect of the Second Noble Truth is to refute the existence of a first cause and also a singular cause.

Everything is unfolding in a cycle, and each thing has multiple aspects.

- Origination supports the very philosophy of interdependency and the law of karma.

- This aspect of origination refers to multiple causes and conditions as well as to interdependency.

- The main object is to refute a first cause and a singular cause.

Q & A

10 minutes: Lead the class through a short Q & A session.

Questions for Review:

- What is the name of the Second Noble Truth?

- How would you describe karma in your own words?

- What types of things are affected by karma?

- How would you describe origination in your own words?

- Why is it important to understand that there is no first cause and no singular cause?

Class Four

Aspects of the Second Noble Truth: Well Produced and Condition

Objectives

Students will:

- Learn the third aspect of the Second Noble Truth: "Well Produced"
- Discover how our past actions lead to suffering
- Explore the fourth aspect of the Second Noble Truth: "Condition"
- Examine the roots of suffering: Ignorance, attachment and aversion
- Discover how Karma affects rebirth

Class Outline

Introduction:

5 Minutes: Begin with a short 5 minute Shamatha meditation.

Lecture

60 Minutes: The third and fourth aspects of the Second Noble Truth: "Well Produced" and "Condition."

Q & A

10 minutes: Lead the class through a short Q & A session.

Lecture on the following points:

The third aspect of the Second Noble Truth has a meaning of "produced" or "well produced."

- This third aspect is to show that whatever we experience is a direct result of our karma.
- When we experience suffering, it is because we have participated personally in the creation of that karma.

Whatever suffering we experience is a direct result of our past actions and emotions.

- Sometimes this extends over multiple lifetimes so it is difficult for us to see how we have caused it.
- It is important to recognize that no one else has produced that karma for us.

When Buddha taught the Four Noble Truths he was refuting all theistic religions.

- He asked the question, "If everything was created by God, then why would a benevolent God create so much suffering?"
- Buddha could not reconcile these opposing factors.

Thus Buddha taught that every suffering we experience, whether it manifests as feelings of pain or of pleasure, must be coming from karma we have personally created.

- In order to prove this, Buddha taught this third aspect of the Second Noble Truth "Well Produced."

"Well-produced" means that due to our own karma we are now experiencing these sufferings.

- It has nothing to do with some other force creating such suffering.
- This is also related with karmic law. Buddha said that whatever we experience has a direct connection to what we have personally done in the past. All results are due to our own karma and our own emotions.

The fourth aspect of the Second Noble Truth: Condition

- There are some religious schools like the Jain that believe we have a permanent soul.
- This permanent soul is said to always be at peace even though circumstantially we have pain and suffering.
- The Jain believe in a soul which is always happy, and which is free from suffering.

To refute such teachings, Buddha taught about conditions.

- He observed that all the experiences we have are not only due to our causes but also to our conditions.

- Causes are like the seed, and conditions are like the water, soil, and everything that makes the seed grow.

Causes and conditions are very much related to each other and determine the result.

- This aspect of condition mainly refutes a permanent cause.
- In this way Buddha is saying that the Second Noble Truth of "origination" or "causation" is a product of causes and conditions.
- As a result of these causes and conditions we experience suffering.

As we have established, the First Noble Truth is the Truth of Suffering which includes all three kinds of suffering.

- The Second Noble Truth examines all of the causes and conditions of that suffering.

There are three main causes of suffering:

- Ignorance, desire, and anger.

It is due to ignorance that we create karma.

- Ignorance is the main cause of birth and rebirth.
- When we die without any awareness or any practice, when we experience overwhelming pain and suffering at the time of death, we tend to lose consciousness.

When the elements of our physical bodies are dissolving at the time of death, we often cannot maintain our awareness.

- That unconsciousness is, in some sense, an experience of that ignorance.
- Because we become unconscious at the time of dissolution, we cannot maintain wisdom, we cannot maintain awareness.

Out of that lack of awareness, out of that unconsciousness, when we wake in the bardo intermediate stage after death:

- The habitual patterns and all the karma that has been impressed on our consciousnesses will take over our minds.
- All of these afflictive emotions that have been imprinted on our mindstreams will follow us into the bardo.
- We will carry very strong desire and attachment after death, which will then force our rebirth.

We are conceived and reborn again and again.

- In that very first moment of conception, when our consciousness is combined with our father's and mother's elements, that is the beginning of the suffering of conditioned nature.
- The very fact of our birth means we will experience old age and death and will experience the suffering of the conditioned nature of all things.

The Buddhist teachings always discuss death as occurring every moment.

- Death is "momentary."
- From the very moment we are conceived we have started toward death because every moment we are changing.

We can experience that impermanence in every heartbeat.

- At any moment the heart can stop, and we can leave this body.

We have evolved to have this physical body that becomes the basis for the other two kinds of suffering.

- We are conceived due to ignorance.
- With conception we have physical bodies.
- Then, with a physical body, we have the three kinds of suffering.

The suffering of suffering and the suffering of change are both based on the suffering of conditioned nature.

- The basic suffering of conditioned existence is there all the time, even when we don't actively feel the suffering of change or the suffering of suffering.

Shantideva taught in the "Bodhicaryavatara," that most anger is rooted in pain and suffering.

- When we have physical pain we may become short-tempered and impatient.
- Often we express this anger to the people we are closest to emotionally.

Pain can make adults act like children again.
- When children have physical pain, sometimes they act it out on their parents.
- Maybe children think they can get away with expressing anger toward their parents since they feel unconditionally loved by them.

It is a common human trait to try to find someone to blame for our suffering.
- We try to find some kind of excuse by becoming angry at outer circumstances or at someone in our lives.

The other obvious source of suffering occurs when our desires are not being fulfilled.
- This may also cause us to become angry.
- The desire is there in the first place because we do not see the true nature of the object of our desire.

Through these examples, we can see how the afflictive emotions are completely interdependent.
- Desire is there because of the ignorance.

- Unfulfilled desire can cause suffering.
- Suffering can be the root of anger. They are all interrelated.

The expression of these three afflictive emotions at a mental level generates karma.
- At the verbal level, when we express these three emotions, that becomes verbal karma.
- At the physical level, when we express these three emotions through actions, that becomes physical karma.

We can see how karma and those destructive emotions are the causes and conditions for the three kinds of suffering.
- The more we understand the way causes and conditions operate, the more we can free ourselves from misconceptions about karma.

On a larger scale, when we accept karma:
- Karma can refute all those big philosophical questions about whether a Creator is responsible for our suffering.

When we take personal responsibility for creating our own karma:
- We can begin to recognize how our karma is creating our experiences of the entire universe.

- This can encourage us to stop blaming outer circumstances and to begin creating causes and conditions for a positive future.

This is not to diminish how interdependent we are.

- Our personal experiences generated by our individual karmas are also affecting the universe.
- For this reason it is very important to understand karma, which includes the six causes, five conditions, and four results.

The Buddha taught that one act of killing can have multiple results.

- One example is that this act of violence may shorten our lives.
- Furthermore, if we kill with desire, like killing an animal for meat, then that type of killing can increase our desire.
- If we kill with anger, then that will increase our anger.
- If we kill with ignorance, that will increase our ignorance.

All these types of killing will also make our habitual pattern of killing stronger.

- As a result, by killing others, by eliminating their lives, we will experience more lifeless situations in our environments.
- It will actually affect the energy of our external world. You can really sense this in areas of war or conflict.

Even one act of killing includes all six causes, five conditions, and four different results.

- Why are there four results? Why are there six kinds of causes?

If we study in depth, then we see that there are many factors involved in even killing one sentient being.

- For this reason, studying the complexities of karma can be very important.
- The more we study, the more we can clear away any doubts and misunderstandings. This in turn will give us more and more confidence about the natural law of karma.

These four aspects of the Second Noble Truth are to clear away all the misunderstandings related with the three sufferings and their causes and conditions.

Q and A

10 minutes: Lead the class through a short Q & A session.

Questions for Review:

- What does "well produced" mean?
- Is it helpful to recognize that our actions contribute to our pain and suffering? If so, how?
- Do the teachings on "conditions" support or refute the idea of a permanent cause? Why is this important?
- On what three levels can we generate karma?

- In what ways might our individual actions influence collective karma?

Class Five

The First Aspect of the Third Noble Truth: Cessation

Objectives

Students will learn:

- The definition of nirvāna
- The fundamental purity of sentient beings
- The differences between nirvāna and drug induced states

Class Outline

Introduction

5 minutes: Begin with a short 5 minute Shamatha meditation.

Lecture

60 minutes: The first aspect of the Third Noble Truth: "Cessation"

Q & A

10 minutes: Lead the class through a short Q & A session.

Lecture on the following points:

The Third Noble Truth is the truth of "cessation."

- This truth acknowledges that there can be an end to suffering and that we can reach nirvāna.

How do you define nirvāna ?

- While we may try to understand nirvāna intellectually, the state of nirvāna is actually beyond our intellect.

- Without a direct experience of nirvāna it is very difficult for us to comprehend what nirvāna is.

- As scholars and practitioners, we will attempt to understand it in order to comprehend the possibility of freedom from suffering.

Example: Sugar

- Only those of us who have tasted sugar will truly know what sugar is.

- We cannot reach this experience through discussion or comparison.

- No matter how many names we use for sugar, nor how deeply we go into describing its chemical properties, we cannot duplicate the experience intellectually.

What is nirvāna ?

- Nirvāna is the cessation of suffering.

- That result can only be reached through practicing the Noble Eightfold Path, which will be presented in the Fourth Noble Truth.

As we have discussed, Buddha gave four different aspects to each of the Four Noble Truths.

- These four aspects are to clear away all our doubts and misconceptions.
- Over the course of the next two sessions, we will cover the four aspects of the third noble truth.

Cessation

- The first aspect of the Third Noble Truth of nirvāṇa is "cessation" which has a meaning of liberation.
- This first aspect helps to clear away any misunderstandings related to whether freedom from suffering is possible.

If we believe that the destructive emotions, which are the cause of all the sufferings, are inherent in human nature:

- Then no matter how much we practice, we will never be free.

If we believe that these afflictive emotions are our true nature:

- Then whatever faith we cultivate, whatever spiritual practice we may do, there will still be no possibility of going beyond suffering and the causes of suffering.

Buddha taught that human beings are fundamentally pure by nature:

- Buddha taught that all sentient beings are possessed of "Buddha nature" and have the potential to become free from suffering and the causes of suffering.

Throughout human history there have been two schools of thought regarding humanity.

- One school thinks that the nature of humanity is passionate and aggressive.

- This school thinks that humans are wired for war and conflict, and that they are imprinted with fight or flight responses, neuroses, and afflictive emotions.

- There are some who would argue that these responses are embedded in our genes and cannot be altered.

The other school of thought, which is shared by Buddhists, is that by nature we are pure, compassionate, and wise.

- Buddhists understand that the nature of life right now is suffering and that suffering has causes.

- Buddhists also perceive that the nature of our minds is free from suffering and free from the causes and conditions of suffering.

- That our inherent nature is actually nirvāṇa.

In the Sutra teachings, that inner space in the mind, that inherent nature, is described as being similar to outer space.

- When we have lots of clouds and bad weather we don't see the blue sky.

- When we have many disturbing emotions and concepts in our minds then we cannot see the clarity of our inner space either.

We can glimpse this inner space through meditation practice. When we have a very good, deep meditation session:

- Whatever is not real, whatever is relative, whatever is fake will temporarily dissolve.
- What remains is the clarity of that inner space.

Outer space is unconditioned:

- It has been unconditioned for an infinite time in the past.
- It will be unconditioned for an infinite time in the future.
- All the planetary systems, billions of them, come and go.

According to the Buddha, these planetary systems are limitless, but none of them are permanent.

- Only space remains because it is unconditioned.

Our earth is just one tiny planet, and humans are only one small fraction of the sentient beings on earth.

- But for us personally, our own experiences are so important that whatever we experience we assume should be a universal truth.

- We think everyone has to agree with us and has to see reality as we see it.
- There is no universal truth to our perceived reality.

What we experience is based on our inner conditions.

- Our individual inner conditions have shaded all of our experiences and have projected a unique experience of the external world.

When we discover that inner space through meditation:

- We transcend all these objects.
- Where the inner space and the outer space become one, our experience of everything changes.

When the inner and outer space merge, then for the first time we have a glimpse of nirvāṇa.

- In addition, we see the absence of all emotions, including the root destructive emotions of anger, ignorance, and attachment.

In this glimpse of nirvāṇa, we see the possibility of complete freedom from suffering.

- However, as long as we have feelings, we have suffering.
- Even a happy feeling is suffering according to the Buddha.
- Even a neutral feeling is suffering.

As we have discussed, when we have pleasure we think we are happy.

- But that is our misunderstanding of relativity and karma.

- Because we experience the result, and we don't see the cause, we think that this is freedom from suffering.

- But even those positive feelings can become a cause for negative feelings.

Example: Here in the west when we hear the word "nirvāṇa" we probably think of Kurt Cobain and his famous band "Nirvana" from Seattle.

- Cobain's life was actually an example of the horrible suffering of samsara.

- He rose to stardom as a very young man.

- He sold millions of records around the world. But his fame and wealth only fueled his addictions and increased his suffering.

Artists and musicians are very creative people. They are very sensitive.

- They work on cultivating through their art an inner space that may even feel like nirvāṇa at times.

- But the method they are applying is often confused, and the attention they receive often serves to reinforce their destructive emotions.

- As a result, they can fall down into terrible suffering.

This is what we do in samsara:

- We try so hard to avoid suffering through false methods.

In the sixties our culture erupted in a positive revolution fueled by drug use.

- Some of these psychedelic drugs had the power to give people a glimpse of nirvāṇa.
- But that high was quickly followed by the withdrawal.

There is no shortcut to nirvāṇa.

- True freedom from suffering can only be reached through deep meditation practice.

Nirvāṇa is *not* a state of feeling.

- Painkillers and recreational drugs have the power to temporarily kill feelings in our nervous systems.
- We may feel some relief, some freedom from suffering, but that is not the same as cessation.

Feeling is based on ego, and when we forget ourselves, we think we are having a wonderful experience.

- But relief is only temporary when it is achieved in this way.
- These drugs are not actually freeing us from any of the underlying afflictive emotions.

Our attention always goes to an area that has pain.

- When we have a headache, all we can think about is that nagging discomfort.
- If our feelings have been hurt by a friend, all we can think about is that rejection.
- However, we generally don't carry as much awareness of areas that are free from pain.

Many of these drugs are a way to forget ourselves.

- Because we feel a temporary relief, we wonder if it is similar to nirvāṇa.
- But being momentarily ecstatic or numb, or forgetting ourselves as a result of a drug, has very little in common with the experience of nirvāṇa.

Nirvāṇa is the awareness of a state beyond feeling.

- The realization of inner space is based on awareness and mindfulness, not distraction.
- When we go beyond the ego and self, we can become free from all of the five aggregates.

Nirvāṇa is the cessation of the five aggregates.

- We go beyond the aggregates of form, feeling, ideation, formation, and consciousness.
- We go beyond our physical bodies. We go beyond our feelings, ideas, and activities.

- In the state beyond ego and self, we experience inner space. When we are fully aware of that inner space, we are experiencing nirvāṇa.
- We are experiencing the cessation of craving and attachment and of all the feelings related with the five aggregates.

"Cessation" means freedom from all the conditioned and unconditioned phenomena.

- It means freedom from feelings, ideas, and activities.
- This includes freedom from our minds and emotions.

Cessation is possible because that inner space is the nature of our minds.

- In that inner space all the aggregates dissolve.

Through meditation practice we can experience this first aspect of the Third Noble Truth, this aspect of "cessation."

- Since we can experience this cessation, then we know there is liberation.
- We know that there is freedom not only from suffering but from the very causes of suffering.

Q & A

10 minutes: Lead the class through a short Q & A session.

Questions for review:

- What is nirvāna ?
- Why do you think that Lama Migmar used the metaphor of sugar when teaching about nirvāna?
- Are the destructive emotions an inherent part of human character?
- Can nirvāna be replicated or experienced by drugs?
- If not, why not?

Class Six

Aspects of the Third Noble Truth Continued:

Pacification, Immaculate, and Going Beyond

Objectives

Students will learn:

- The differences between therapeutic meditation practices and practices that bring liberation
- A brief introduction to the heavenly realm and the formless realm
- Deeper dimensions of nirvāna

Class Outline

Introduction

5 minutes: Begin with a short 5 minute Shamatha meditation.

Lecture

60 minutes: Second, Third, and Fourth Aspects of the Third Noble Truth: Pacification, Immaculate, and Going Beyond

Q & A

10 minutes: Lead the class through a short Q & A session.

Lecture on the following points:

The aspect of cessation that we have discussed last class can be very useful in combatting our worldly narcissistic ways of life.

- It can refute those who don't have any faith in spiritual enlightenment and liberation.

While the Buddha didn't face as much materialism or capitalism as we experience today, there were five prominent non-Buddhist philosophers in India whose misconceptions he was working with.

- In particular, there was one non-Buddhist school called "Charvaka" that was very similar to many of our materialistic societies.
- The Charvakas only believe in this one life. They don't believe in rebirth or karma. Their main purpose in life is to be narcissistic and to pursue pleasure.

The Indian philosopher who founded the Charvaka school had a very clever mind.

- He developed this whole theory that there is no rebirth, and there's no karma whatsoever.
- He thought this pursuit of pleasure was what our lives were comprised of.

Humanism is currently becoming more popular here in the United States.

- Humanists do not have faith in anything which they cannot see or prove.

- If they don't see rebirth, they cannot believe in it. Everything has to be proven based on direct experience.

Many of us have not seen India yet, but we believe it exists because others have been there.

- Among the Humanists, there is no belief in any inferential logic.

- Even today, Buddha's ancient teachings can help to refute these new belief systems which don't subscribe to karma or rebirth.

The second aspect of the Third Noble Truth is called "pacification." We may practice meditation for any number of reasons.

- Meditation in the Western world is often used for therapeutic purposes.

- If we practice according to Herbert Benson, we are practicing for the relaxation response.

- If we practice meditation according to Jon Kabat-Zinn, then the goals of meditation may be mindfulness based stress-reduction.

If we practice shamatha meditation, then maybe we will experience some peace, but this doesn't mean that our peace is permanent.

- Even the best shamatha practitioners only achieve awareness and freedom from actively destructive emotions.
- However, shamatha meditation still doesn't free us from sleeping emotions.

We often misunderstand peace as being equivalent to nirvāṇa.

- However, nirvāṇa is an unconditioned state.
- It's a permanent state.
- Even if we experience peace for one whole lifetime, that doesn't mean that we have reached a state of nirvāṇa.

Nirvāṇa is unconditioned, and it is a permanent state once we achieve it.

- The aspect of pacification makes it clear that these temporary peaceful experiences of meditation, like that state of meditative absorption in the form and formless realms, are not nirvāṇa.

If we are successful in cultivating a good shamatha meditation, that meditation can help us experience a more peaceful mind.

- If that shamatha is not integrated with mindfulness meditation, then when we wake up from that shamatha we are still prone to destructive emotions and suffering.

This second aspect, "pacification," is to clarify that those temporary peaceful states achieved in shamatha meditation are not equivalent to nirvāṇa.

According to Buddhist cosmology, gods such as Brahma, are part of the form realm.

- Merit accumulated through acts of love, compassion, joy, and equanimity can help someone to be reborn in the form realm.
- Some levels of the form realm are called the abode of the Brahma, the "Brahmaviharas."

Someone who has practiced these virtuous qualities without much wisdom:

- Will have a better chance of being reborn in the form and formless realms.

Within Buddhism the form realm is also called the heavenly realm.

- But that heaven is not a Buddha realm.
- That heaven has not gone beyond samsara.

- Those heavenly beings have been reborn there due to lots of merit and positive karma, but still they are missing the wisdom that transcends samsara.

These beings have peace, pleasure, and happiness.

- However, peace and happiness are not nirvāṇa. Nirvāṇa is an unconditioned permanent state of cessation.

The third aspect of the Third Noble Truth is called "immaculate."

- This aspect also signifies accomplishment.
- When we achieve that inner space of nirvāṇa permanently,
- that state is immaculate because we have transcended even the causes and conditions of suffering.

This third aspect is also a clarification on formless beings.

- Yogis who have more merit are reborn in the form realm and the heavenly realm, which we have just discussed.

Meditators who are even more accomplished are reborn in the formless realm.

- But both the form and the formless beings are still not liberated. They are still not beyond samsara

In the formless realm, beings do not have physical bodies.

- They don't have pain or pleasure, happiness or unhappiness.

- They only have neutral mental feelings and very subtle concepts in the mind.

For this reason, meditation is much deeper in the formless realm.

- It is a state of absorption, free from all active and gross feelings and thoughts.
- In the formless realm, the mind maintains a level of attention.
- This state of absorption is also called "samadhi."

This third aspect of the Third Noble Truth is to clarify that such states of absorption are not nirvāṇa.

- Even if formless beings were to remain in samadhi for eons, when they emerged from meditation, suffering could still arise.
- In this state they could still experience disturbing emotions.
- This experience of absorption is not an unconditioned state.

Only nirvāṇa is immaculate, pure, and unconditioned.

The fourth aspect of the Third Noble Truth is "going beyond" or "renouncing" samsara.

- Samsara is the endless cycle of life and death that we experience.

- This cycle of suffering is depicted by the Buddhist image of the Wheel of Life.

Samsara is not limited to our small planet earth.

- Due to our karma and emotions, we are reborn again and again in the desire, form, and formless realms, throughout countless planetary systems.

Nirvāṇa is when we go beyond the samsara of these three realms.

- It is full renunciation.
- As long as we experience feelings of any kind, even of profound peace, we are still not in a state of nirvāṇa.

It is only when our spiritual practice and meditation have the power to go beyond samsara's three realms:

- That we will we experience the complete cessation of suffering.

As long as we have an ego, we cannot go beyond the three realms.

- Ego causes the emotions of ignorance, attachment, and anger to arise.
- Out of these root destructive emotions, we create so much karma.

Due to interdependency we are cycling again and again through countless lifetimes.

- Only when we see the true nature of ego, only when we are egoless, will we be free from destructive emotions.

As long as we are attached to ourselves, we won't have renunciation.

- Only when we reverse the Wheel of Life, only when we overcome ignorance through deep meditation, can we achieve nirvāna.

Buddha taught these four aspects of the Third Noble Truth in order to clear away all the misunderstandings and doubts about nirvāna.

- Nirvāna is reached through the Noble Eightfold Path presented in the Fourth Noble Truth.

Q & A

10 minutes: Lead the class through a short Q & A session.

Questions for Review:

- How does nirvāna differ from the peaceful states that are experienced in mindfulness based stress-reduction practices?
- Is nirvāna a permanent or an impermanent state?
- Is the experience of Samadhi (absorption) the same as or different from nirvāna?
- Why is nirvāna considered to be immaculate?

- What role does renunciation play in the achievement of nirvāna?

Class Seven

Aspects of the Fourth Noble Truth:
Seeing Selflessness and Suitability

Objectives

Students will learn:

- A brief overview of the Eightfold Noble Path
- The path of accumulation and application
- The four levels of the path of application
- The first and second aspects of the Fourth Noble Truth: the path of "seeing selflessness" and "suitability"

Class Outline

Introduction

5 minutes: Begin with a short 5-minute Shamatha meditation

Lecture

60 minutes: The first and second aspects of the Fourth Noble Truth: Seeing Selflessness and Suitable

Q & A

10 minutes: Lead the class through a short Q & A session.

Lecture on the following points:

The Fourth Noble Truth is the Noble Eightfold Path.

- This path leads to self-awakening and ultimately to the cessation of suffering.
- It offers us eight principle guidelines to live by.

These eight guidelines include:

- Right view, right intention, right speech, right action, right livelihood, right effort, right mindfulness, and right concentration.

"Path" in this context has a meaning of realization based on our practice.

- Generally in Buddhism, we refer to five different levels of the path.
- This starts with the path of accumulation that begins when we take refuge.

In the path of accumulation

- We accumulate merit by doing our practices again and again.
- These practices can be related with meditation or with keeping precepts, or be based on wisdom trainings.

By practicing repeatedly, we counteract negative karma and the actions which cause destructive emotions.

- Through the path we come to the result that is the state of nirvāṇa we have just discussed.

The second path is the path of "application."

- As our practice becomes stronger and stronger, we can overcome negative actions and destructive emotions more easily.

Within our minds, there is always a conflict between positive and negative emotions and actions.

- Before we develop a spiritual practice, our destructive emotions and negative karma are often strongest.
- These negative emotions and actions form habitual patterns and also determine our personalities.
- But once we commit to the spiritual path, our positive karma and positive emotions grow stronger and stronger through our practice.

The path of application has four different levels. These four levels are:

- Heat, summit, patience, and excellent Dharma.
- These levels are the measurement of how much merit we have accumulated and how much negative karma we have burned and purified.

When our accumulation of merit becomes very strong, and we burn off all our negative karma, we may see a glimpse of selflessness, a glimpse of emptiness.

- That glimpse is our entry into the path of seeing.
- The Noble Eightfold Path, which is the essential feature of the Fourth Noble Truth, is part of the realization of the path of seeing.

When a yogi has a glimpse of emptiness, of selflessness, then for the first time wisdom can arise.

- That realization can happen only when we have purified our negative karma and overcome our active destructive emotions.
- Only then may we have a glimpse of emptiness.

The first aspect of the Fourth Noble Truth is the path of "seeing" the emptiness or selflessness.

- Based on this insight, we continue to see that emptiness or selflessness more and more in our meditation.

This glimpse of emptiness gives us profound understanding and faith in the path.

- It invigorates our practice since we become absolutely convinced that we can achieve the result— nirvāṇa.
- It also helps us to overcome any misconceptions and any false belief in a permanent self.

When Buddhist yogis glimpse the truth of selflessness, they become utterly confident that there is no such thing as a permanent self.

- The nature of the self is selflessness.

- This is very critical, critical not only philosophically, but also critical in proving that there is nirvāṇa, which is the cessation of the self.

This cessation of the self includes the cessation of all five aggregates as well.

- Even the fifth aggregate, which is the mind and mental consciousness, is also ceased.

When all these defiled aggregates are ceased, then a yogi will not perceive any permanent self.

- What is realized instead is the wisdom of selflessness.

- Only the wisdom remains.

This is why the Noble Eightfold Path is important.

- As we have discussed, there are five levels to the path.

- There are the two worldly levels of accumulation and application, and then there are three noble levels.

When we speak of these levels in the context of the Fourth Noble Truth, we are generally referring to those three noble levels.

- These levels are the path of Seeing, the path of Meditation, and the Path of No More Learning.

The first worldly level, accumulation, is about recognizing the path.

- This brings us confidence that there is a way forward which can help us realize nirvāṇa.
- We realize that through the second worldly level of application we can apply the dharma practice and gain insight.
- This paves the way for the three noble levels of the path: the path of seeing, the path of meditation, and the path of no more learning.

The spiritual path is not a linear trajectory.

- Rather, it is a progression through different states of mind.
- The path is a method to evaluate and guide our realizations.

The second aspect of the Fourth Noble Truth is "appropriate" or "suitable."

- Whenever we have a certain realization in the mind, this aspect helps us to see what is possible and what is not possible.

- For example, when we glimpse our own selflessness, then we see that selflessness is possible and that self-clinging is not appropriate.

If we look within the mind, there are things to be abandoned, and there are things to be realized.

- But these things are still within the mind.
- When we go beyond the mind, there is nothing to realize.

Even if we study Buddhist psychology according to the two levels of the Abhidharma, the study still cannot encompass all the complexities of the mind.

- The mind is very intricate and filled with contradictory thoughts and emotions.
- Love is in the mind. Hate is also in the mind.
- Both of these mental states exist, but the two are completely opposite.

The same is true with jealousy.

- Jealousy is there, and joy is also there.
- All the conflicting emotions are there. There are destructive feelings, positive feelings, and neutral feelings.

As we follow the Buddhist path, we start to understand that spiritual practice helps us to abandon many negative activities and mental states.

- Through this process of abandonment and renunciation, we start to make space for great realizations to occur.

Q & A:

10 minutes: Lead the class through a short Q & A session.

Questions for Review:

- What is the path of accumulation?
- Why is repeated practice important in the path of accumulation?
- How does the path of application differ from the path of accumulation?
- Why is an insight into selflessness important with respect to the Fourth Noble Truth?
- Why is it important to recognize what is "appropriate" or "suitable?"

Class Eight

Aspects of the Fourth Noble Truth Continued: Achievement and Liberation

Objectives

Students will learn:

- What achievement means in the context of the practice
- The differences between the three vows: Pratimoksha, Bodhisattva and Samaya
- The meaning of permanent deliverance

Class Outline

Introduction

5 minutes: Begin with a short 5 minute Shamatha meditation.

Lecture

60 minutes: The third and fourth aspects of the Fourth Noble Truth: "achievement" and "liberation."

Q & A

10 minutes: Lead the class through a short Q & A session.

Lecture on the following points:

As we have discussed, if we study all the mental activities according to the ancient Buddhist texts of the Abhidharma:

- We will learn that there are ten basic natural activities of the mind that are always present.
- There are also negative emotions like ignorance and attachment.
- And positive emotions of love and compassion.

Buddhist practice relies on cultivating positive emotions.

- Through focusing on positive emotions, we learn to gradually overcome the negative ones.
- We are working towards uncovering the natural qualities of the mind which are wisdom and compassion.

This aspect of "suitability" means that emotions and mental activities are not permanent.

- They are there to be transformed.
- Through the practice we abandon that which is to be abandoned, and then we begin to see the inherent qualities of the mind.

The mind is very complex. We need the mind in order to accomplish our spiritual journey.

- Ultimately, through practice, we can achieve nirvāṇa, that state in which the mind ceases to exist.

You may wonder what is left after the mind ceases?

- When we go beyond the mind, only wisdom remains.

This second aspect of "suitability" or "appropriateness," informs our practice.

- As we progress along the spiritual path, we can use this aspect to determine what must be abandoned and what can be achieved.

The third aspect of the path is "achieving" or "attaining."

- When we talk about achievement in this context, we don't mean achievement on a mental level.
- What we are really talking about is achievement based on wisdom, based on recognizing the true nature of the mind itself.

As we abandon more and more negative activities and emotional states, we begin to achieve this inherent wisdom.

- The second aspect we just discussed of "suitability" has more to do with method, with the means of accomplishing.

This third aspect "attainment" is about achieving nirvāṇa.

- We are practicing in order to achieve freedom from suffering.

- When we go beyond the mind, we call this "achievement" or "attainment."

This accomplishment is very different from the way we think of achievement in our ordinary lives.

- Through abandoning all our negative karma and destructive emotions, we can discover the very nature of our minds.
- Uncovering that wisdom is the extraordinary "achievement."

The Four Noble Truths are primarily taught in the Hinayana tradition of Buddhism.

- According to this tradition, nirvāṇa is the ultimate accomplishment.
- The Four Noble Truths have also been adopted by the Mahayana and the Vajrayana traditions of Buddhism

In these traditions, the ultimate goal is quite different.

- The Mahayana tradition puts great emphasis on the Bodhisattva path.
- In the Bodhisattva path, we aim to free not only ourselves but all beings from suffering.
- We take the Bodhisattva vow stating that we will continue to take rebirth in order to help others.

The ultimate achievement in both Mahayana and Vajrayana is full enlightenment.

- Full enlightenment is not the same as nirvāṇa.

- Nirvāṇa is the accomplishment of wisdom alone.

- Full enlightenment includes compassion.

According to the Mahayana and Vajrayana traditions:

- Enlightenment is the union of both wisdom and compassion.

The results of our practice will be determined by whatever vows we have taken.

- The Hinayana vow of Pratimoksha emphasizes self-liberation as the ultimate state.

- If we take that vow, we can achieve liberation in nirvāṇa.

In the Mahayana tradition, we take the Bodhisattva vow.

- We promise to practice for the sake of all sentient beings.

- Due to this vow we can achieve full enlightenment, the union of wisdom and compassion.

- When we achieve full enlightenment, we effortlessly reincarnate in order to continue to help other beings.

Vajrayana practitioners take the Samaya vow.

- The Samaya vow cannot be taken without the Pratimoksha and the Bodhisattva vows.

- Vajrayana encompasses all three vows.

When we achieve the stage of a "yidam," a fully enlightened being, then we have the same power to effortlessly manifest to help other sentient beings.

- The only difference between the Mahayana and Vajrayana is the path.

- Vajrayana offers us more elaborate and varied practice methods than Mahayana does.

The resulting enlightenment, however, is basically the same.

- This third aspect of the path, the aspect of "achievement," will differ based on the Buddhist path we practice and the vows we take.

The fourth aspect of the path is "liberation" or "permanent "deliverance."

- Through our diligence and practice, the path has the power to deliver us to complete freedom from suffering and the causes of suffering.

The term "deliverance" in this context also means cessation.

- In this final stage, we go beyond all karma and emotions.

- The path has the power to free practitioners completely from suffering and the causes of suffering.

Q & A

10 minutes: Lead the class through a short Q & A session.

Questions for Review:

- Why does the Buddhist path emphasize the cultivation of positive emotions?
- What remains after the mind ceases?
- What is achieved or attained in the third aspect of the path?
- How does the ultimate goal in the Hinayana tradition differ from that of the Mahayana and Vajrayana?
- What is the Bodhisattva vow?

Class Nine

The Noble Eightfold Path: Right Views Part One

Objectives

Students will learn:

- How the first right view is wisdom
- The fault in seeing the five aggregates as the self
- Why believing in Karma is fundamentally important for those on the spiritual path

Class Outline

Introduction

5 minutes: Begin with a short 5 minute Shamatha meditation.

Lecture

60 minutes: The third and fourth aspects of the Fourth Noble Truth: "achievement" and "liberation."

Q & A

10 minutes: Lead the class through a short Q & A session.

The Fourth Noble Truth is the Noble Eightfold Path leading us from suffering.

- This path has eight factors which can guide us on the way.

The first branch is Right View, which is the most important part of the Noble Eightfold Path.

- It is the most important because Right View is related to wisdom which overcomes ignorance.
- In order to realize Right View we have to investigate the wrong view.

Buddha taught that there are five wrong views:

- Wrong views are those misconceptions through which our defilements are increased.

The first wrong view is seeing the five aggregates as the basis of the self.

- The first wrong view has a meaning of projecting ego onto the five aggregates.
- We project some inherent permanence of the self and ego onto these five aggregates of form, feeling, ideation, formation and consciousness.

The first Right View: Selflessness of Self and Phenomena

- To counter the first wrong view of "satkayadrsti," Buddha offered the first right view of the selflessness of oneself and phenomena.

We all cling very strongly to the self and ego.

- Some masters emphasized that the source of suffering in samsara is this attachment.

- They observed that first we cling to the self; then we cling to all the objects we possess, whatever we call "mine" in our universe.

- With these two wrong views of "self" and "mine" we produce very strong clinging, and all our destructive emotions are increased.

Those who are on the path of seeing will see that this clinging to the self and to the five aggregates is only relative.

- It is not an ultimate truth.

- We are born with an ego, and we spend much of our lives reinforcing that ego.

- Yogis who are on the path of seeing realize that the ego is just a relative projection.

As we look deeper and deeper on the path of seeing, we begin to have a glimpse of emptiness for the first time.

- In this glimpse we realize that what we have projected is only relative; it is not inherently existing.
- Ultimately we cannot find any permanent self.
- We begin to realize that we cannot find any inherent existence in the five aggregates.
- That's why all these projections are part of a wrong view.

If we look for a permanent self in each of the five aggregates, we cannot find any proof.

- When we study the great teachings of "The Heart Sutra," we see the nature of the five aggregates.
- The Sutra says, "Form is emptiness, emptiness is form; form is no other than emptiness, emptiness is no other than form."

In this way the Sutra breaks down all our assumptions about the five aggregates.

- When we look closely at the first aggregate of "form," from the gross level of the human body, right down to the cellular or atomic level, we cannot find the self.
- When we look into the second aggregate of "feeling," we also cannot find a self.
- When we examine the third aggregate of "ideation," we also cannot see any inherently existing self in all our thoughts.

If we continue on to the fourth aggregate of "formation," we learn that there are over fifty different kinds of mental activities included in this aggregate.

- Even if we look into every single one of them, we cannot find any evidence of a self.
- Even if we look into the mind, into that fifth aggregate of "consciousness," we cannot find the self or ego.

Due to our strong emotions, we become incredibly attached to our sense of self.

- If we look closely at our lives, we begin to see how much energy we invest in building up and protecting this ego.
- We are projecting a self, interdependently, based on the five aggregates.

Only through meditation, when we see the emptiness in all five aggregates, will we also see the true emptiness nature of the self.

- Whenever we project a sense of self, it is actually a wrong view.
- Wrong view is having emotional involvement with a sense of self in reference to the five aggregates.
- Buddhists would consider the Hindu belief in a permanent self or "atman" to be a wrong view.

Now on the other hand, when we see selflessness for the first time, then we understand right view.

- In order to know what right view is, we need to fully recognize our wrong view.
- Wrong view includes not only belief in the personal self but also all of our self-references.
- This includes all of the objects which we consider "mine." We can only own something if we believe we exist in the first place!

This involvement with our possessions is also based on the five aggregates.

- This applies to all of our attachments, material and mental, related to this idea of "mine."
- We say "my car" or "my child" or "my country," and we believe that all of these are existing in relation to ourselves.

Until we see the emptiness in all the phenomenal objects, as well as in ourselves, we will still be trapped in our wrong views.

- For this reason Buddha taught the selflessness of the person and the selflessness of phenomena.
- Yogis and meditators on the path of seeing recognize the inherent selflessness and emptiness of all things. This is the first right view.

Second Right View: Belief in Karma

- To counter the second wrong view of "mithyadrsti," we must first examine our misunderstandings related with karma.
- We may talk about karma all the time, but there are many misconceptions.
- We don't see the truth of cause and result. We often overlook the interdependency between cause and result on the relative level.

Of course ultimately things are beyond interdependency.

- There are two levels to everything, the relative level and the ultimate level.
- Every object has relative interdependency and ultimate emptiness-nature.

Take a bell for example: A bell has relative interdependency.

- There are causes and conditions that produced the bell, but the true nature of the bell is emptiness.

There are two aspects to each object.

- What we will see is dependent on how we are looking into that object and on the level of our meditation experience.

If we don't believe in interdependency on the relative level, then we don't believe in karma.

- Not believing in karma cuts all the roots of our virtues and merits.

- If we don't believe in cause and effect, then we have no motivation to increase our positive activities.

- It is vital to our spiritual practice that we recognize the truth of interdependency in the relative world.

Without belief in karma, there is a risk that we will become nihilists.

- In the Buddha's time, in India, there were some non-Buddhist schools that did not believe in karma.

- As a result, they also did not believe in rebirth.

- Buddha taught about karma in order to counter these misconceptions.

As I have mentioned, the very reason the Charvaka philosophy was developed was to permit people to indulge their appetites and to become more narcissistic.

- According to that philosophy even killing or stealing is permissible in the pursuit of pleasure.

- There is no belief in karma, therefore, the Charvakas have no concern about the consequences of their actions.

- They believe only in momentary feelings and in whatever actions will bring them pleasure.

The Charvakas are known to be the most narcissistic philosophers.

- Buddha taught this second right view in order to help lift their ignorance regarding karma.

Failure to believe in karma is the second wrong view.

- We live in the relative world. We live in interdependency.
- We must go through the interdependency in order to see emptiness.
- If we don't believe in interdependency, then it is unlikely we will realize emptiness.
- It is also unlikely that we will cultivate all the positive spiritual qualities and good merit necessary to gain realization.

Belief in interdependency and karma has to do with natural law.

- If we don't believe in natural law, then there is disharmony on a fundamental level.
- If we don't believe in karma, we will also not believe in rebirth.
- If we believe that we are only living for this one lifetime, then we will have very little incentive to accumulate merit or to do virtuous deeds that don't immediately benefit us.

Q & A

10 minutes: Lead the class through a short Q & A session.

Questions for Review:

- What wrong view does "selflessness of self and phenomena" counter?
- Why is it wrong to project the ego onto the five aggregates?
- Why is it important to believe in Karma?
- How does interdependency relate to Karma?
- What two aspects does every object have?

Class Ten

The Noble Eightfold Path: Right Views Part Two

Objectives

Students will learn:

- The detriments of holding extreme views
- The purpose of Buddhist scholarship
- The inexpressible nature of wisdom

Class Outline

Introduction

5 minutes: Begin with a short 5 minute Shamatha meditation.

Lecture

60 minutes

Q & A

10 minutes: Lead the class through a short Q & A session.

Third Right View: Freedom from Extreme Views— to counter the third wrong view of "antagrahadrsti"

- We can use our understanding of the interdependency of the relative world to see the ultimate truth of emptiness.

- It is a right view if we also use emptiness to understand that we live in interdependency in a relative world.
- Only through truly understanding relativity will we see emptiness.

This is the reason why we have to do all this accumulation of merit and the preliminary Ngondro practices.

- The Ngondro practices are based on karma.
- We accumulate good karma in order to purify negative karma.
- The ultimate aim is to go beyond karma altogether to see emptiness.

The third wrong view is when we have extreme views about our own conclusions.

- If we have concluded, through study and analysis, that our philosophical stance is superior, then we become attached to that conclusion.
- It is a wrong view to believe that our ideas are the best.

This is the fundamental problem at the root of religious extremism and fanaticism.

- Terrible atrocities have been committed throughout history based on the belief that "my God is better than your God."
- Many wars have been fought in order to defend a belief that "my view is the best."

We can find these extremes in religion and within various philosophical schools.

- Within Buddhism, we have four philosophies: Vaibhasika, Sautrantika, Mind Only, and Madhyamika.
- Each one of these philosophical stances can lead a philosopher to an extremist position.

This is a danger within all the Tibetan traditions.

- There are many debates among philosophers.
- These philosophers have all determined that their own conclusions are the best.

This is also a great danger for Buddhist scholars.

- This intellectual attachment to particular views can often be a huge impediment to meditation practice.
- This kind of extremism may help to spread knowledge and scholarship, but it can be counterproductive to spiritual practice.

The purpose of Buddhist scholarship is threefold: study, reflect, and practice.

- Practice must free us from extremism and liberate us from all of this clinging.

If we are clinging to the very method that we are using to liberate ourselves, then that is one of the worst attachments.

- It can prevent us from any true realization.

Sometimes the best scholars have the biggest egos.

- This is true in religion and in academia.

- If scholars have not used that knowledge to transform themselves, if they have not seen the wisdom within all the ideas they have collected, then there is very little growth and realization. They become trapped by their own intellects.

This is why we have so much fighting over the "isms."

- We see this conflict between all the religions as well as between communism and capitalism.

- All these "isms" have something to do with coming to a particular conclusion.

If we become very attached to a particular conclusion, then there is the potential to become extreme.

- We can become extreme in our views based on either eternalism or nihilism.

Within theistic religion, eternalism can be a great danger.

- This is where we see the view that, "My God is the supreme God. My God is the best."

- We bring God into the realm of our own egos, projecting a sense of ownership over God.

As a result we find any opposing view to be a direct threat.

- This is how we decide that "my God is the only God. Your God is the bad one."
- We are fighting over God. Would God really want it that way?
- We lower God to our level, and basically this becomes a fight of the ego!

Buddha warns us against any extreme view.

- Even atheism can become an extreme view.
- Humanists in New York recently bought a billboard in a Jewish Orthodox neighborhood and wrote in Hebrew saying something to the effect of "your God is just a myth."
- These same Humanists also bought a billboard in New Jersey and wrote a similar message in Arabic, insulting the Muslims. So we see that even the Humanists can fall into an extreme.

If we are attached to "our" God, we don't realize that we don't know who God really is until we are very enlightened.

- Until then our egos are making God something very permanent. As a result we are waging war and fighting constantly.

Eternalism can be a wrong view.

- Nihilism is also a wrong view. This absence of belief in anything is equally extreme.

Within any of the Buddhist philosophies, if someone thinks his or her view is the only "right one," then in reality it is a wrong view.

- Tibetans think they have the highest and best Buddhist philosophy "Madhyamika."
- Within the highest Madhyamika, then the Tibetan scholars debate which conclusion is the best between "self-emptiness," "other emptiness," and "emptiness free from the four extremes."
- This argument has lasted for many centuries and it still continues today.

Scholars cling to their own views. Those who believe in "other emptiness" think they are the best.

- Those who explain emptiness according to "freedom from the four extremes" think they are the best.
- There are three groups even among the Tibetan schools. It's an ongoing argument.
- The great yogis, the great meditators, are focused on their practice and really don't worry about these arguments.

The third wrong view is extremism.

- This is the wrong view of being an extremist who clings to a particular conclusion of an opinion or idea.
- Yogis who are gaining realization on the path of seeing realize that ultimate reality is free from all the extremes.

Buddha reiterated again and again that wisdom is inexpressible.

- Wisdom is beyond words, beyond expression.
- Most of the time we will fall into one of the extremes the moment we try to express wisdom through words.

If we read all the Sutras, we even find contradictions in Buddha's teachings.

- This is a result of Buddha teaching to a particular audience at a particular time.
- He would teach in a way that was most appropriate to those in attendance.

That's why there were said to be three turnings of the wheel.

- This was a graduated path, designed to lead people slowly towards some understanding.
- Buddha knew that if he explained emptiness to people who had no other Buddhist foundation, that the truth of emptiness could be very shocking and terrifying.

- Buddha realized that people might even become too frightened to practice.

That's why Buddha's teachings lead us step by step.

- When describing ultimate reality, Buddha said it's free from all the extremes.
- We cannot express this ultimate reality, but it is something we can realize through great practice.

For those who have realized ultimate reality, that wisdom cannot be expressed.

- Understanding freedom from the four extremes is the best reference we can have for that experience.
- The reference cannot give us the experience.
- Only meditation can offer us this realization of wisdom.

Clinging to any of the four extremes of existence, non-existence, both or neither, is the third wrong view.

Q & A

10 - 15 minutes: Lead the class through a short Q & A session.

Questions for Review:

- Why do we focus on cultivating good Karma?
- What is the ultimate aim of Ngondro practice?
- What is the threefold purpose of Buddhist scholarship?

- Why is it wrong to think that our conclusions are the best?

- What are some of the dangers of extremism?

Class Eleven

The Noble Eightfold Path:
Right Views and Right Intention

Objectives

Students will learn:

- The importance of not clinging to spiritual practices or philosophical views
- The importance of right intention
- The roots of anger, and why it's necessary to overcome it

Class Outline

Introduction

5 minutes: Begin with a short 5 minute Shamatha meditation.

Lecture

60 minutes

Q & A

10 minutes: Lead the class through a short Q & A session.

Fourth Right View:

- Not esteeming our own spiritual practices and disciplines as the supreme

To counter the fourth wrong view of "shilavrataparamarsha" we should be careful not to cling to, nor esteem, any of our practices as being supreme.

- Whether we have taken Pratimoksha vows, or Bodhisattva vows, or Samaya vows, we must be very careful not to think that our disciplines are the best.
- Practice and discipline should be methods to go beyond the emotions.
- If we get too attached to our methods, then they will not liberate us.

Buddhists who are doing a daily sadhana meditation practice can contemplate these questions:

- Why do we do the generation stage practice?
- After reciting the mantra, why do we then have to do the completion stage practice and meditation beyond thought?
- Why can't we just stay in that deity's form?

We have to go beyond that subtle attachment to the divine and to the form of the deity we are practicing.

- That's why we must do the completion practice.

- If we get too attached to the method and to the deity, then that method can actually increase our egos.

Instead of helping us to become free and liberated, our practice can bind us.
- That's how it can become a wrong view.
- We will never realize the path of seeing if we are too attached to our practices.

Fifth Right View:
• Not esteeming our own conclusions or views as the supreme.

To counter the fifth wrong view of "drstiparamarsha," one should not think or esteem one's own conclusions or views as being the best.
- One Tibetan scholar said, "In the end, we become extremists because we draw philosophical conclusions based on our extreme attachments which are rooted in the ego."
- This implies that no matter how much we study and practice, until we are enlightened we will only have a limited understanding, and thus we will still fall into an extreme.

Knowledge is based on ego. That's why knowledge is not wisdom.
- We bring our understanding to these studies at the level of our egos, and then we get attached to those views.

- Then we use the philosophies of Tibetan and Indian Masters and of the Buddha himself to substantiate our views.

- None of this is based on our own realization and liberation.

When scholars do academic research, they sometimes talk about uncovering "original" truths related to Buddha's teachings.

- How original are these truths? In the context of their research studies it is based on ego more than on enlightened wisdom.

Intellectual study is based on relative information and knowledge.

- We present some new findings, and then we believe that what we have done is authentic and original.

- None of these academic findings are based on wisdom.

- They are based more on research into the material relative world and on synthesizing information from various places.

- Our own extreme attachment to a conclusion can be a wrong view.

We have to recognize the five wrong views in order to correct them.

- Through our meditation practices we move beyond the paths of "accumulation" and "application" to reach that third path, the path of "seeing."

- On this path of "seeing" we understand our wrong views and finally have a glimpse of Right View.
- This is called "noble view" because for the first time we have achieved some realization on the path of seeing.

Until then, these five views may be merely intellectual.

- We may contemplate them rigorously, but they are still not noble because they are tainted with the ego.
- Because they are tainted with the ego, they have the potential to increase our defilements.

Only after we reach the path of seeing, do these views become noble.

- Now our seeing has the power to defy not only the active destructive emotions but also those latent or "sleeping" destructive emotions.
- For the first time we will truly understand this first and most important branch of the Noble Eightfold Path, the branch of Right View.

Right Intention is the Second Branch of the Noble Eightfold Path.

- Intention is very important. Intention in combination with volition is the beginning of all karma and all action.
- Intention starts in the mind, and then through volition that intention is connected with an object.

- This is how our intentions become active.

As long as we are in samsara, we have not seen the path of seeing or beyond.

- We still struggle with the three root afflictive emotions of desire, anger, and ignorance.
- Even when we are feeling peaceful and content, those destructive emotions are still "sleeping emotions" in our consciousness.

Just because we aren't actively engaged in a destructive emotion, doesn't mean that it's not still in our subconscious and able to arise at the slightest provocation.

- When we investigate this second branch of the Noble Eightfold Path, we realize that sleeping anger resides in us constantly, even when we are not actively experiencing it.
- Sleeping anger is activated when our wrong intention becomes volition. We direct that anger toward our enemy or toward some object.

Intention has two potentialities:

- It can be wrong or right, depending on how it arises.
- Intention is related with mental karma or mental activities, which we call "sems-byung" in Tibetan.

If we look within the mind, we begin to see that the mind has many mental activities:

- Some scholars translate these activities as emotions. But the Sanskrit word is "chitta," stemming from the word "chit" that means mind.

Mind is a general word we use for what is actually a composite of many different activities.

- These activities can be divided into three categories: positive, negative, and neutral mental activities.

In the higher Abhidharma teachings there are fifty-one mental activities described.

- In the lower Abhidharma there are forty-six mental activities.

Mind is not just one single independent entity. It is composed of many factors:

- Due to volition, mental activities are activated.
- Through volition our anger becomes directed to an object that we consider an enemy.
- When this occurs we may feel like our entire mind is anger.

Anger arises because there is also an element of desire operating.

- Maybe that person we don't like, who has now become our enemy, is somehow obstructing our desire and depriving us of what we want.

Ignorance is also present in anger.

- When the dominant afflictive emotion is anger, we may only recognize that one emotion.

Overcoming anger is one of the primary Right Intentions.

- There are many spiritual practices designed to help us overcome anger.
- Developing bodhicitta and loving-kindness can be a great antidote to anger.

An angry mind is always activated to harm someone or something through speech or physical actions.

- Meditations on love and compassion, and especially on cultivating bodhicitta, can help us to generate positive emotions towards others.

"Harming" refers to how much physical or mental suffering we create.

- "Helping" is defined by how much happiness and pleasure we can bring to another being.

- The Buddhist understanding is that as long as we have love and compassion and bodhicitta, then we are helping others to feel more happiness and to develop the causes of happiness.

If we don't develop these positive qualities, we will continue to experience hate instead of love.

- We will feel passion instead of compassion.
- Without the cultivation of bodhicitta, we will experience self-clinging.
- These negative emotions of hate, passion, and self-clinging create tremendous conflict between ourselves and others.

As long as our egos are not fulfilled, we will want to harm others because they are not letting us have what we want.

- This is why taking the Bodhisattva vow is so important to our spiritual transformation.
- The Bodhisattva vow helps us to correct our intention and motivation.

If we don't take a strong resolution such as the Bodhisattva vow, then our intention remains harmful.

- We may not recognize this because it is so subtle.
- If we are attached to ourselves, we will continue to be competitive and to place our own desires above others.

That attachment to the self will extend the territory of the ego further and further into the universe.

- In some sense, everything becomes a threat to our sense of self.
- When this egotistical attitude reaches an extreme, we see people in power willing to kill thousands and destroy whole countries in order to extend their territory.
- This is a magnification of the ego and anger.

Buddha gave us practices like bodhicitta to counter these wrong intentions. Any practice we undertake has to start with the mind and mental activities.

- This is especially true with regard to Right Intention.
- When we can overcome our anger in the mind, we can generate Right Intention.

Right Intention is the beginning of all wholesome karma.

- Wrong intention, based on anger, is the root of all harmful activities.

Q & A

10 - 15 minutes: Lead the class through a short Q & A session.

Questions for Review:

- Why must we not esteem our practices as supreme?
- How does knowledge differ from wisdom?

- Why are intentions important?

- How are mental activities activated?

- What additional emotions are present in anger?

Class Twelve

The Noble Eightfold Path: Right Intention

Objectives

Students will learn:

- How precepts can help us overcome ignorance, anger and desire
- The importance of right intention
- The importance of renunciation
- Why these truths are called "Noble"

Class Outline

Introduction

5 minutes: Begin with a short 5 minute Shamatha meditation

Lecture

60 minutes

Q & A

10 minutes: Lead the class through a short Q & A session.

The Importance of Taking Precepts and Vows:

Taking resolutions and honoring precepts are a vital antidote to wrong intention.

- "Path" has a meaning of practice and transformation.
- Transformation has to take place at the very core.
- Taking resolutions help us to correct our motivation on the deepest level.

Most of the time we are not aware of our sleeping emotions.

- If we are not actively experiencing anger, we may deny that we have any anger at all.
- Anger still exists silently in our minds.
- If we take the precept of overcoming any negative actions, this helps us counteract the roots of that anger in the mind.

The physical and mental precepts we take are disciplines.

- How quickly these disciplines serve as antidotes to negative emotions depends on the strength of our habitual patterns.

If we are people who are used to expressing anger and being violent, then when we take a precept not to kill, it may be very challenging at first.

- These habitual patterns of anger are as strong as any other addiction in the mind.

If we are addicted to alcohol or drugs, then when we make resolutions to quit those addictions, it will be extremely challenging in the beginning.

- In the case of alcohol, repeated intoxication has created a systemic dependency.
- When we first deprive the body of this substance, it may be very uncomfortable.
- Even if we try to detox from caffeine, the withdrawal may give us a terrible headache and make us exhausted.

The discomfort of detox is a result of how these substances have become part of our entire physical bodies.

- In a similar way, when we first try to overcome the destructive emotion of anger, we may be surprised by the strength of that habitual pattern.
- It is very difficult to begin cleansing our minds of that addiction.

Overcoming Anger, Desire, and Ignorance:
When we operate in certain ways for years and years, our habitual patterns become so strong that we mistake them for our personalities.

- We may start to believe that we are wired to have a short temper.
- We may claim that we are "just emotional and passionate by nature."

If we do anything with enough repetition, we begin to believe it is a fixed personality trait.

- These negative habitual patterns become mental addictions very easily.

- We begin to believe that this is who we are by nature and that it is not in our control to change.

Most of the Buddhist precepts we take are to counteract these patterns of thought and action.

- In the beginning this may feel like a very artificial repression of emotion but eventually these antidotes will begin to break down the roots of our sleeping emotions.

Our experience of *active* anger may feel like the most challenging emotion to overcome:

- It is actually the subtle *sleeping anger* which is hardest to uproot.

Active anger exists because we have this sleeping aggression deep down in our minds.

- When we can begin to access these more subtle levels of emotion, we can break down the root causes of this anger.

It is vital that we honor our precepts and vows:

- This discipline is essential to the work of deep transformation.

- Overcoming anger is a vital component of Right Intention.

The other very important aspect of cultivating Right Intention is overcoming desire.

- As we have discussed, anger and desire are very dependent on each other.
- We become angry when our desire is not fulfilled.

When we don't get something we want, or when something threatens our egos, we have pain and anger.

- These emotions are all mixed together.

As long as we have sleeping ignorance, we will also be subject to all five of the wrong views we discussed previously.

- Although ignorance is the most difficult sleeping emotion to recognize because it is so subtle, it is still considered a *primary* cause.

Overcoming ignorance is also included in Right Intention. When we take precepts, we are correcting three unwholesome or non-virtuous mental actions.

- The first is "coveting," which is related to desire.
- The second is a "harming mind," which is related to anger.
- The third is "wrong view" which is related to ignorance.

This second branch of the Noble Eightfold Path is primarily concerned with ways to overcome the harmful mind of anger and its corresponding emotion of desire.

- Overcoming desire is vital to our transformation, especially because we humans are living in the desire realm, and everything we consume is based on attachment.

If we examine all our feelings of happiness and pleasure, we realize we are often operating with very conflicting intentions here in the desire realm.

- We may say that we act virtuously in order to have happiness and pleasure, but even that intention is not pure.
- It is still very relative. That happiness and pleasure-seeking is still rooted in feelings of desire and self-clinging.

The Importance of Renunciation

If our virtuous activities are focused on attaining happiness and pleasure, then that result is not perfect.

- When we look closely, we see that pleasure always becomes the cause of future desire.
- Since that pleasure is not permanent, the minute it fades we have a strong desire to experience it again.

Momentary happiness becomes the cause and condition of more desire.

- The more we consume, the more our appetite grows here in the desire realm.

- This is the reason why renunciation is so strongly emphasized in Buddhist practice.

- Renunciation is key to overcoming our desires.

In the graduated path, whether it is in the Hinayana, Mahayana, or Vajrayana Buddhist practices, renunciation is essential.

- Why is renunciation so important? Because renunciation is our first step in gaining some freedom from desire.

Desire creates many challenges in our meditation practice.

- The moment we want to focus on one object of meditation, a desirable object will often show up in our minds instead.

- When our desire is not fulfilled we become angry or irritable.

Desire obscures our ability to see reality clearly.

- As long as we have desire, we never see the true nature of an object.

- We will romanticize one object; we will reject another object.

- We will bring all these conflicting emotions into our meditation practices, and they will obscure our vision.

Cultivating renunciation is essential in our practice. This is the reason why we take all these precepts.

- The precepts are presented in terms of renunciation: no killing, no stealing etc.
- We are trying to refrain from those actions and those emotions.

Once we have taken the precepts, then each time we refrain from a negative activity, we are actually cultivating positive qualities.

- Right Intention begins with renunciation.
- If we are on the Mahayana path, then we also take the Bodhisattva vow and cultivate love and compassion for the sake of all sentient beings.

Right Intention and Karma

Right Intention is so important because it is the beginning of all karma.

- Karma is multidimensional and very complex.
- Karma starts with our intention and volition.
- If we change our intention, then we begin to transform our karma.

For a yogi who has reached the path of seeing, the intention is noble because it is free from both anger and desire.

- At this point the yogi has seen the wisdom.

- Once we have seen wisdom, we have overcome ignorance, and most actions will become noble.

Right View and Right Intention help us to overcome all the root mental negativities of ignorance, anger, and desire.

- Ignorance by itself, anger by itself, and desire by itself are not karma.
- When they are drawn towards an object by intention and volition in the mind, they become action.

This action is harmful when it is rooted in the afflictive emotions, and then it becomes part of our karma.

- We need to make the distinction between emotions and actions.
- It is important to examine them separately, as well as to look at what happens when they are combined.
- Buddha's teachings help us to better understand how and why we are acting and feeling in certain ways.

We observe our actions at the verbal and the physical levels of expression. We don't look deeper to see the roots of our intentions.

- Intentions are often overwhelming and blinding to us.
- Intention is the root of action. When defilements and emotions are directed toward objects by volition, then they become karma.

Right View and Right Intention, the first two branches of the Noble Eightfold Path are both related to mental actions.

- They describe the right mental actions and offer insight into overcoming wrong mental actions.
- Buddhist practice involves taking vows and precepts to counteract the destructive emotions and their causes.

Q & A

10 - 15 minutes: Lead the class through a short Q & A session.

Questions for Review:

- Why do we take precepts and vows?
- What three primary mental states do precepts and vows help to overcome?
- What role does intentionality play in our emotional reactions?
- Why is renunciation important?
- How could becoming more aware of intentions and actions help to benefit you and others?

Class Thirteen

The Noble Eightfold Path: Right Speech

Objectives

Students will learn:

- The detriments of idle chatter
- Why to avoid harsh speech
- The importance of telling the truth

Class Outline

Introduction:

5 minutes: Begin with a short 5 minute Shamatha meditation.

Lecture

60 minutes

Q & A

10 minutes: Lead the class through a short Q & A session.

Right Speech

The third branch of the Noble Eightfold Path is Right Speech.

- In order to understand Right Speech, we have to learn how to overcome wrong speech. Buddha taught four categories of wrong speech.

Idle Chatter

The first category is idle talk.

- This means useless trivial chatter without much meaning
- This chatter arises from unfiltered thoughts and concepts

If we have a lot of inner chattering inside our own minds, we may feel the need to express it verbally.

- This expression may give us some relief.
- Trivial conversations don't do anything fundamentally transformative.
- Useless chatter is like watching an entertaining movie. It's just another way of trying to forget or deny other feelings by distracting ourselves.

Idle chatter may be temporarily enjoyable, but idle conversation is actually a waste of our energy.

- Buddha preferred to do meditation.
- Buddha maintained a noble silence. That's why Buddha's name was "Shakyamuni. "Muni" means "silent one.""

We meditate in silence because it helps to quiet the chattering inside us.

- Talking activates certain parts of the brain that may not be conducive to meditation.
- If we talk a lot during times when we are not practicing meditation, it can impact the quality of our minds.

Idle talk is considered wrong speech because it is just a waste of our effort.

- Useless chatter becomes the source of lots of emotions and concepts.
- Often we speak before we think, and this can be harmful to others.

Talking gets us into lots of trouble! Talking also includes so much affirming and negating that we are led into extremes of thinking.

- There is a story of the Buddha that illustrates this point.
- The story deals with the famous Fourteen Questions which the Buddha didn't answer.

There were fourteen questions that Buddha refrained from answering.

- Buddha knew that regardless of whether he answered "yes" or "no" he could somehow mislead the questioner toward a wrong conclusion.

Talking gives rise to many emotions in ourselves and in others.

- If we can try to talk less and less, and maintain that noble silence, we will experience more peace.

In order to counteract this form of wrong speech, we can strive to have meaningful conversations and to only speak when it is necessary and useful.

- We can choose silence instead of trivial chatter.

Lying is another form of wrong speech.

- The obvious antidote to lying is to always tell the truth.
- Karma is still in the realm of relativity. It is not a perfection. For this reason there are exceptions where telling the truth can be too harmful.

Only when we are like Buddha, and we know everything, will we know what is truly helpful.

- If lying brings pain and suffering, then we must counteract that by telling the truth.

A third action we must avoid is harsh speech.

- Buddha always emphasized speaking gently.
- Speaking harshly actually increases anger, and it can be very harmful to others.

- Speaking gently is very important to maintaining Right Speech.

The fourth action to avoid is speaking deceptively.
Deception here has a meaning of misleading others.

- We may inflate some story in order to benefit ourselves.
- Saying things with the intention of personal gain, whether it's fame, power, attention, or wealth, is all considered deceptive speech.

Right Speech and the Ten Non-Virtues
The path of Right Speech helps us to overcome all the negative karma that is motivated by destructive emotions.

- Right Speech means avoiding all of those four types of wrong speech.
- Those four types of wrong speech are included in the natural law of the ten non-virtues.

The ten non-virtues include three mental non-virtues, three physical non-virtues, and the four verbal non-virtues which we have just discussed.

- The fact that speech has the most non-virtues attached to it is a reflection of how much karma is produced by our verbal actions.
- Our karma is primarily created through our speech.

The extent to which physical actions affect others is fairly limited.

- It is limited because the target of those physical actions has to be near us to feel the effects.
- Speech can reach much further than physical actions, and as a result it can create so much more karma.

We can call someone who lives in India on the telephone, and we can yell at them or lie.

- We can be deceptive or speak harshly. It's hard for us to hit someone in India from here!
- Speech, however, is very powerful. That's why there are four non-virtues that involve speech.

We need to maintain Right Speech for as long as we can.

- The more meditation we do, and the more we maintain a noble silence, the better chance there is that all four negative aspects of speech can be overcome.

Most of our social interactions are based on speech.

- The more we can pray or chant or meditate, the more we can counteract these four aspects of wrong speech.

We have now discussed the first three branches of the Noble Eightfold Path:

- These include Right View, Right Intention, and Right Speech.

- We have covered all the wrong actions related with the mind and all the wrong actions related with speech.

Q & A

10 minutes: Lead the class through a short Q & A session.

Questions for Review:

- In what ways would avoiding idle chatter be beneficial?
- For the majority of the time, it's best to avoid lying but life isn't always black and white. Can you think of examples when telling the truth could be harmful?
- In your view, what are some of the potential detriments of harsh speech?
- What are some of the benefits of avoiding deceptive speech?
- What are the first three branches of the Noble Eightfold path?

Class Fourteen

The Noble Eightfold Path: Right Action

Objectives

Students will learn:

- The importance of avoiding killing
- How right action applies to all living beings
- The importance of the middle way
- Why we should avoid stealing

Class Outline

Introduction:

5 minutes: Begin with a short 5 minute Shamatha meditation.

Lecture

60 minutes

Q & A

10 minutes: Lead the class through a short Q & A session.

The fourth branch of the Noble Eightfold Path is Right Action. This means refraining from wrong actions.

- Killing is a wrong action.

- Killing includes even the smallest insect.

As a society we presume killing always has to do with anger.

- In reality we probably kill more from desire and ignorance.
- We've created an entire meat industry out of our desire for certain foods.
- Back in the primitive world, we would hunt for just enough food to feed ourselves, but the modern world is very different.

Documentaries on the current meat industry show the shocking treatment of animals.

- Today we have corporate industrialized killing of great numbers of sentient beings.
- The animals in these factories suffer terribly.
- When we sit down to eat at our tables, we rarely think of where the meat comes from and of how inhumane the conditions were for the abused animals.

Right Action is not just about action related to humans.

- Right Action is also about how we treat animals and other beings.
- We kill many beings through our desire and ignorance.

Right Action has to do with overcoming our wrong actions with regard to all sentient beings.

- These wrong actions, such as killing, can arise from any or all of the three destructive emotions of desire, anger, and ignorance.
- Regardless of which destructive emotions are involved, killing is wrong as far as karmic law is concerned.
- Karmic law has nothing to do with the laws of a particular country.

Even within Buddhism, depending on our practice and on how many precepts we have taken, there are different consequences.

- As far as natural law is concerned, any actions we do based on the destructive emotions are considered wrong actions.

Wrong action is not just related to other sentient beings.

- Wrong action can also apply to inanimate objects.
- For example, a wrong action would be to misuse something that is not ours.
- It is even possible to commit wrong actions with objects that we own.

Right Action involves finding some kind of middle path.

- Buddha's life is a good example of finding a middle path.

- For six years Buddha lived as an ascetic. He starved himself and meditated.
- His strict discipline and deprivation did not allow for very high realization.

At the end of his sixth year, a girl from the nearby village offered him some rice pudding.

- When Buddha tasted the rice pudding his meditation experience became stronger.
- In this moment he recognized that it is better to maintain a *middle way* on the spiritual path.

We cannot become too extreme in our actions.

- Even if we own something, we should be careful not to misuse it.

Most actions are expressions of emotion.

- If our expressions serve to increase our destructive emotions, we need to change how we relate to an object.
- If we deprive ourselves of something, and if our minds are not strong, then this can increase our pain and generate more anger.

Deprivation can create many emotions for people who are poor.

- If we do not have many material things, if our basic needs are not being met, then deep down we may carry resentment towards those who are wealthy.
- We see these class struggles throughout history.

Abundance can also create many emotions for people who are wealthy. Indulgence can make people more narcissistic.

- Our appetites can become insatiable.
- We are always craving more.
- Neither extreme will bring us into the middle way.

This fourth branch of the Noble Eightfold Path shows us:

- Any actions that help us overcome our destructive emotions have the potential to increase positive things.
- Any actions that increase our destructive emotions are potentially wrong actions.

How we own things and what we own are also part of Right Action.

- This is very controversial.
- As a developed society, we have a sense of entitlement based on artificial systems.
- These systems don't have any intrinsic value. The value is only projected.

The only intrinsic value is what is directly related to sustaining our lives.

- We place a great deal of importance on money, as if that alone were keeping us alive.
- Without air, without earth, or water, or energy, or soil, money would be worthless.

Money does not actually keep us alive.

- If we cannot breathe, then no matter how much money we have, we cannot live.
- Our entire society is based on artificial projections of value.
- Society has convinced us that we need many things.

The former prime minister of Malaysia, Dr. Mahathir, says that our present economic system is really just high stakes gambling.

- The stock market probably deals with billions of dollars every day, but nothing is getting produced through the stock exchange.
- Traders are buying and selling billions of dollars, but there is nothing tangible to show for this.
- It's all just numbers and projected values.

Dr Mahathir said that as long as we keep operating this way, our economy will always be at risk.

- It's just legalized gambling.

- He suggested that everyone who is trading stocks could produce something instead.

- According to what is produced, they would get a return. They could live on such a return.

- If we try to live based on gambling monies, then someday we may lose everything.

- We have already seen Wall Street suffer major losses in the past.

This leads us to the topic of stealing.

- If we look into it more deeply, we come to understand that whatever we use that we don't own is actually a form of stealing.

- If we own something but we misuse it or waste it, then in some sense we are depriving others of these resources.

- With every liter of gas we use, we are essentially taking the earth's energy.

It is important to connect our consumption to cultivating positive emotions.

- Every time we eat food, we should bring some purpose to why we are eating.

In Buddhist food-offering prayers it says very clearly, "I'm not eating this food out of desire, out of anger, out of ego or pride. I'm eating just to sustain my physical body with the

essence and nutrients my body requires, so that I can do practice and positive deeds."

- We should learn to approach everything we do in our lives with this clarity of purpose.
- If we have altruistic goals, then there is more justification for our use of resources.
- If we are living just to eat, then what is the difference between humans and animals?

Sakya Pandita said in his Elegant Sayings that wild animals spend their whole day looking for something to eat.

- Animals are just focused on basic survival.
- What is the difference between animals and humans?

There is no difference if we too are living only to consume.

- If we live so that we can do something beneficial for ourselves and others, then we are engaging in Right Action.
- Right Action includes our attitude toward all the things we consume.

Another important aspect of Right Action is how we act in our interpersonal relationships.

- How we conduct ourselves with regard to others is incredibly important.

- If our relationships are based on strong destructive emotions like anger and desire, then we can become obsessed or aggressive.

Good relationships depend on how many positive qualities of mind we bring to one another.

- Qualities such as love, compassion, and forgiveness have far more potential to create and sustain positive relationships.

Right Action includes all of the physical actions.

- We try to bring some positive emotions and awareness into everything we engage with through our senses.
- Whether it's what we look at, what we hear, what we smell, or what we eat, we try to bring some positive qualities to this experience.

Right Action has to do with how we conduct ourselves physically in relation to all sentient beings and to all objects.

Q & A

10 minutes: Lead the class through a short Q & A session.

Questions for Review:

- Why do you think that we should avoid killing ALL sentient beings?

- What are some examples of how Right Action can be practiced in relation to objects?
- Why is it important to find a "middle way?"
- Does the teaching on non-stealing apply to the objects that we own? If so, in what ways?
- How can we practice Right Action in our relationships?

Class Fifteen

The Noble Eightfold Path: Right Livelihood and Right Effort

Objectives

Students will learn:

- The different types of wrong livelihood
- The definition of right livelihood
- How taking precepts can help us focus on positive activities
- The three wrong mental karmas

Class Outline

Introduction

5 minutes: Begin with a short 5 minute Shamatha meditation.

Lecture

60 Minutes

Q & A

10 minutes: Lead the class through a short Q & A session.

The fifth branch of the Noble Eightfold Path is Right Livelihood.

- Any livelihood that cultivates more destructive emotions in ourselves and others is considered wrong.
- Right Livelihood should be something that is ethical, humane, and that cultivates more positive qualities within us and within others.

Buddha specifically described four wrong livelihoods. The first wrong livelihood is selling intoxicants like alcohol or drugs because these increase our ignorance.

- Intoxication can deprive people of their mindfulness, their attention, and their conscious discernment of what is right and wrong.
- Selling intoxicants is actually one of the most negative livelihoods.

Cultures promote drinking as part of the social fabric.

- In Tibet they drink this home-brewed drink called "chang."
- Chang is used to celebrate or to forget pain and suffering.
- Slowly it becomes the cause of many other problems, and we see an increase in addiction.

Drugs are also very detrimental.

- Engaging in selling drugs is a wrong livelihood because drugs completely cloud a person's mind.

- Drug users lose the ability to discriminate between what is right and what is wrong.
- There are many drug-induced crimes.

The second wrong livelihood Buddha described is that of being a butcher.

- Any worker in a modern slaughterhouse could be said to have wrong livelihood.
- The more meat eaters there are, the greater the demand for meat will be.
- We essentially create more killers.

Killing is taking another life forcefully.

- Due to that unnatural death there is so much pain.

Why does someone become a butcher, and why does that person kill?

- There is desire involved, even if it's just for material gain, just for a paycheck.
- Killing of animals or any sentient beings is very heavy karma.

The third wrong livelihood that Buddha described is dealing in the manufacture and sale of weapons.

- In Buddha's time maybe that just pertained to bows and arrows and cruder weapons.
- These days weapons have become massively destructive.

- Nuclear bombs have the potential to destroy the planet so dealing in weapons is very destructive.
- It creates lethal karma by inflicting so much pain and suffering.

The fourth wrong livelihood Buddha described was the trafficking of humans.

- This applies to the slave trade, prostitution, and any violation of human rights.
- This wrong livelihood produces incredibly heavy karma.

There are also more subtle types of wrong livelihood.

- Teachers have to be very careful. My teacher used to say, "If you become a teacher and a faith object, then people will make offerings to you. If you misuse those offerings that will produce very heavy karma."

- Buddha said in the Sutras, "If people offer something to you out of faith, and you misuse the offering, that is such heavy karma to digest that you will need steel teeth to chew those offerings!"

Any livelihood we have that is beneficial for us and beneficial for others is Right Livelihood.

- Whenever a livelihood becomes harmful to oneself and others, then that is considered a wrong livelihood.

- These are some aspects we have to attend to very carefully on the spiritual path.

In Buddhist understanding, as long as we live in accordance with the natural law of karma:

- Our positive actions and intentions will create more positive karma. We will be in harmony with nature, and as a result there will be more peace in our lives.

In modern civilization, the way we live is regulated by government statutes.

- These statutes are not necessarily always ethical, but most of the time the natural laws are incorporated into the state and federal laws.
- We will need to follow these laws unless they openly oppose our spiritual ethical vows and precepts.

Taking precepts can help protect us.

- Taking precepts are a way of creating very good ethical protection through abiding by the natural karmic laws.
- As a by-product, these precepts can help us live in accordance with state and federal laws. For example, drinking may be legal, but driving drunk is highly illegal.
- Through our precepts of refraining from drinking, we automatically protect ourselves from breaking the laws against drunk driving.

Even though we take the precepts, we are still human, and sometimes we make mistakes.

- In Buddhism there are many confession and purification practices to correct our motivation and renew our vows.
- There are general confession practices, and in the higher teachings we have Vajrasattva purification practices.

It is always better to take the precepts, even if we sometimes make mistakes.

- It's better that we make the resolution to become stronger, even if we sometimes fail along the way and need to recommit ourselves.

Taking precepts is important and beneficial.

- Taking the precepts helps us maintain positive actions.

All of the Pratimoksha vows are designed as antidotes and guidelines.

- Right View and Right Intention are related with mental action.
- Right Speech is related with verbal action.
- Right Action and Right Livelihood are related with physical action.

The Noble Eightfold Path has been perfected by those noble yogis who have realized the path of seeing.

- We are not at that level yet.
- We still need to admit that we have many wrong views, wrong intentions, wrong actions, and wrong habits of speech, and then we have to apply the antidotes for how to correct them.
- Taking the vows and making positive resolutions are fundamental to creating this transformation.

Right Effort is the sixth branch of the Noble Eightfold Path.

- Right Effort can also be translated as Right Diligence.
- To know this sixth branch we have to reflect back upon the previous five branches of the Noble Eightfold path.
- Right Effort is about integrating all those other branches into our lives.

This was also true of the first branch Right View.

- We have to know what all the wrong views are in order to understand what Right View means.
- In a similar way, it is important to understand all the other paths in order to practice Right Effort.

As we have discussed, Right View and Right Intention are related more with mental actions and mental karmas.

- Right View is very connected to Right Intention because our view effects all our thoughts.
- Intention starts in the mind.

There are three wrong mental karmas:

- These are wrong views, the harming mind, and coveting.
- Those are related with the three fundamental destructive emotions of ignorance, desire and anger.

Ignorance is related to wrong views.

- Even if we have cultivated lots of intellectual ideas, if our conclusions are wrong, they are still part of ignorance.

Desire and anger are related to wrong intentions.

- A state of mind that is desirous, harmful, or coveting, is arising from wrong thoughts or mental actions.
- When we are free from these three destructive emotions, we will have Right View and Right Intention.

Q & A

10 minutes: Lead the class through a short Q & A session.

Questions for Review:

- What are the four types of wrong livelihood?
- Why do you think these types of work should be avoided?
- How do we determine what is considered a Right Livelihood?
- What are the three types of wrong view?
- What are some of the benefits of avoiding these three?

Class Sixteen

The Noble Eightfold Path: Right Effort Continued

Objectives

Students will learn:

- The importance of putting our energy into beneficial things
- Why the karmic connection to a teacher matters
- The benefits of faith

Class Outline

Introduction:

5 minutes: Begin with a short 5 minute Shamatha meditation.

Lecture

60 minutes

Q & A

10 minutes: Lead the class through a short Q & A session.

In contemplating Right Effort, it is important to remember all the aspects of wrong speech:

- These include lying, idle chatter, and harsh words.

- We must also remember all the wrong actions and the wrong livelihoods.

Right Effort means increasing our right activities on all three levels: mental, verbal, and physical.

- We increase our Right Effort at the mental level when we cultivate right thoughts.
- We increase our Right Effort at the verbal level when we strive to cultivate right speech.
- We act with Right Effort at the physical level when we perform right deeds.

The Sanskrit word for "Right Effort" is "virya."

- Virya is part of the practice of the six perfections, and it has a deeper meaning.
- It implies that enthusiasm for wholesome activities is considered Right Effort.
- Whenever we engage diligently in positive activities, we help to free ourselves from the negative karmic actions at the mental, verbal, and physical levels.

Right Effort is essential to the process of transformation.

- This transformation happens at a very individual level.
- Whether we will enjoy wholesome activities is dependent upon our habitual patterns.

- If we have been enjoying all the wrong activities, then we have created habits that are very hard to break.

For example, if someone has become a pathological liar it will be very difficult for that person to say something truthful.

- If people have engaged in killing for long periods of time, they can become very cold-hearted. They may not even feel any remorse when they kill.

These negative patterns become entrenched in us.

- How long have we been thinking certain thoughts?
- How are we accustomed to speaking, and what are our physical tendencies?

According to these habitual patterns, our personalities will be formed.

- At a certain point we may even believe that these personalities are our true natures.
- When we first try to counteract these tendencies, we may find it very challenging and stressful.

For example, the first time we do meditation it can be physically and mentally painful!

- Our minds are not used to a meditative state.
- We are met with a waterfall of chattering thoughts and feelings.

- Our bodies may be very restless and uncomfortable when we first try to sit still.

- In order to transform ourselves we need to begin with right effort.

How do we cultivate the energy to meditate?

- Most of our enthusiasm is cultivated based on what we enjoy doing.

- If we like doing something, we will sacrifice everything to pursue it.

- We may even risk our lives to get to the top of the Himalayas or to travel deep into the oceans.

- It may be very difficult to cultivate an interest in meditation.

How do we create the energy to do wholesome things?

- This is our challenge.

- If we are used to doing all the unwholesome activities, engaging in wrong speech and negative deeds, then how can we make that shift?

Meeting a teacher is critical to beginning that transformation.

- We have to meet a guru or mentor with whom we feel a strong connection.

- Or be drawn to a temple or inspired by a teaching.

- Something has to happen to activate our effort.

Buddhists call this resonance with a teacher or temple a "karmic connection." That is where our spiritual journey begins.

Buddha said there are five powers, and the first power is faith.

- When we have faith, it can generate more effort.

Effort is the second power.

- We can see this among yogis and meditators.
- Those who have strong faith can recite mantras all day long, or even meditate in a small cave for years.

In the beginning, faith might not be based on any knowledge or wisdom. It may just be blind faith similar to when we fall in love with someone, but it has the power to increase our effort.

- When we first fall in love with someone, we may think about that person constantly.
- Our feelings are very powerful, and we may even lose ourselves in that love.

That feeling of falling in love is very similar to that first feeling of blind faith.

- The only difference is that on the spiritual path, the object of our love is pure.

When we fall in love with the Dharma, when we fall in love with Buddha, when we become devoted to our gurus, then that love becomes faith.

- That karmic connection to the teacher or to the Dharma is very important.
- In the beginning we might not know who Buddha is or what the teachings are about.
- Maybe we don't have any meditation experience. But if we feel a strong connection to a teacher, it will generate effort.

If we have not made such a connection, then how will we be inspired to pursue the teachings?

- Karmic connection, or whatever term we prefer to use for that feeling of inspiration, is the beginning of cultivating our effort.
- Only when we meet a spiritual person, or when we go through a life-changing event, will we pay attention and pursue the teachings.
- Otherwise it is difficult to break out of our habitual patterns.

The more we pursue the teachings, the more interest and attention we will have.

- As we cultivate a relationship to a spiritual teacher, we will study that teacher's actions, and we will investigate the truths of the teachings.

If the truth resonates in us, and if we trust that we have met a true teacher, then we will begin to emulate these spiritual qualities.

- As our blind faith wears off, if we discover that we do not trust this path or this teacher, we will break away from this relationship.

If our faith remains strong, it deepens our effort.

- Through meditation and study we will begin to know more about the Buddha, the Dharma, and the Sangha. The more we learn about these truths and qualities, the more we aspire to find these qualities in ourselves.

This is the stage where our "blind faith" becomes "unshakeable faith."

- At this stage we have tested the methods.
- We have observed the teacher for a period of time.
- We have used our brains as well as our hearts.
- Now our emotions of faith and our intellectual reason have come together to give us real conviction.

When faith and reason are combined they produce an unshakeable faith.

- Unshakeable faith helps us to have Right Effort.
- We begin to completely devote our lives to wholesome activities of body, speech, and mind.

Unshakeable faith doesn't mean that we are perfect.

- We may still have many imperfections, but the strength of our faith begins to transform our lives on every level.

- At this stage, no matter what happens, nothing will turn us away from our faith in the teachings.

Until our faith is unshakeable, we are operating on blind faith that is based on feelings.

- Our feelings and circumstances are changing constantly.

- That's why we are so fickle in so many environments and relationships.

- We keep changing things in our lives in the pursuit of something better.

- We move from one house to another, one relationship to the next, but still we are carrying our same emotions, and we are restless.

When we have developed unshakeable faith, we naturally want to cultivate more and more wholesome actions.

- Whether it is wholesome thoughts, wholesome speech, or wholesome deeds, we want to focus on these positive efforts.

- We especially want to cultivate those good qualities which have not yet arisen in us.

As we begin to feel the benefits of wholesome activities, our enthusiasm increases.

- The more positive our efforts become, the more we break the old negative habitual patterns.

- These positive efforts will prevent future unwholesome actions from arising.

If we look honestly into our minds, into our thoughts, our speech, and our physical actions, we see how conflicted we really are!

- Maybe sometimes we tell lies even though we want to be honest.

- For whatever reason, there is a habitual pattern to tell lies that we fall into.

If we look closely at our relationships, we also see that it is very possible to love and then hate the very same person or object.

- Love and hate go together. Why is this conflict there?

Since the day we were conceived, and throughout our entire lives, we will experience these dualistic feelings of pain and pleasure, love and hate, attachment and aversion.

- That's why we are never at peace.

Although all we truly want is peace, we remain very restless because we are always moving between extremes.

- We are never in the center.

- That's why faith is one of the most important energies we need in order to cultivate Right Effort.

Through our spiritual practice, our blind faith has to become clear faith.

- Our clear faith can then become unshakeable faith.
- Ultimately we have to develop faith based on wisdom.
- When faith is based on wisdom, it is incredibly powerful.

In the Sutras, Buddha taught that as long as we are here in samsara, conflicted by attachment and aversion, then the universe will not seem perfect.

- If we are always looking for perfection outside ourselves, we will not find it.
- Faith can help us connect to the positive side of any object.
- That's why some masters say, "Faith is like a magnet that will attract all the positive things."

As we develop more and more faith, faith has the power to transform our minds.

- For this reason faith is one of those mental factors that has the most power to cultivate Right Effort.

Q & A

10 - 15 minutes: Lead the class through a short Q & A session.

Questions for Review:

- On what three levels should we increase Right Effort?

- Why should we focus on positive activities?

- What role does faith play in the practice of Right Effort?

- How does blind faith become unshakeable faith?

- What is the most powerful type of faith?

Class Seventeen

The Noble Eightfold Path: Right Effort and Right Mindfulness

Objectives

Students will learn:

- The four aspects of right effort
- The three categories of the Noble Eightfold path
- Mindfulness of the body

Class Outline

Introduction:

5 minutes: Begin with a short 5 minute Shamatha meditation.

Lecture

60 minutes

Q & A

10 minutes: Lead the class through a short Q & A session.

Traditionally we are taught that there are four different practices related to Right Effort.

The first aspect of Right Effort is to develop faith.

- We try to abandon all our negative habitual patterns at the mental level, verbal level, and physical level.

- This is the reason why the preliminary Buddhist practices emphasize accumulating so many repetitions of mantras.

- We have to repeat our practices over and over again in order to break unwholesome habitual patterns.

The second aspect of Right Effort is about strengthening ourselves to prevent future unwholesome actions from arising.

- After abandoning unwholesome patterns in our mental continuums, we then have more power to avoid future negative actions.

The third aspect of Right Effort is about increasing any positive actions we are performing at the mental, verbal, and physical levels.

- We try to cultivate these positive activities until we achieve some perfection.

The fourth aspect of Right Effort is about locating the positive qualities that are not yet being cultivated.

- We then put effort into nurturing and further developing those positive qualities.

The Noble Eightfold Path can be divided into three categories:

- These categories are the training of wisdom, the training of discipline, and the training of meditation.

- As we have discussed, Right Effort is important because it integrates all the other branches of the Noble Eightfold Path.

Right View and Right Intention are part of the training of wisdom.

- As we have established, wrong view is ignorance.

- To counteract that ignorance we need the training of wisdom.

- Right View is an antidote to ignorance. Ignorance is the most fundamental destructive emotion we have.

Right Speech, Right Action, Right Livelihood and Right Effort are all part of the training of discipline.

- This is about disciplining the mind, disciplining the speech, and disciplining the physical actions.

- Discipline is when we make a resolution not to commit negative actions with our body, speech, and mind.

There are many discussions about the human tendency to engage in negative activities and about how to develop ways to stop such tendencies.

- The training of discipline is about refraining from those activities.

- Discipline is an antidote to the destructive emotion of desire.

Right Mindfulness, and Right Concentration, are considered part of the training of meditation.

- These are antidotes to anger, which is the third destructive emotion.

The seventh branch of the Noble Eightfold path is Right Mindfulness.

- Right Mindfulness is divided into the Four Foundations of Mindfulness.
- These Four Foundations are: mindfulness of the body, mindfulness of feeling, mindfulness of mental consciousness, and mindfulness of mental phenomena.

To understand Right Mindfulness, we need to understand the nature of all conditioned things.

- The Buddha categorized conditioned things into the five aggregates: form, feeling, ideation, formation, and consciousness.

The first foundation of mindfulness is mindfulness of the body.

- Mindfulness of the body corresponds with the first aggregate of form or matter.

- All material things are composed of elemental atoms of earth, water, fire, and air.

Whatever is created from these atoms is called "matter."
- Our physical bodies are also composed of these elements.
- We interact with the world around us through our six sense organs.

These are called sense organs because through them we can perceive the entire material world.
- Because we have an eye organ, we can see visual objects. Whatever we see is matter.
- Because we have an ear organ we can hear sounds. Sound is also matter.
- Everything we can smell and taste and touch with our bodies is matter.
- The sixth sense organ of the mind and mental consciousness also perceives phenomena in the material world.

There are many ways to study matter.
- Biologists and chemists examine the components of matter.
- Physicists study matter and it's motion through space and time.
- The Buddhist way of studying matter is to intellectually study its properties and then to use meditation to overcome all of the emotions related with matter.

Whatever sensory objects we experience, through our sense organs and through our minds, become the causes and conditions for different emotions to arise.

- When we see something agreeable, we are attracted to it, and we get attached.
- When we see something repulsive, it gives us pain and suffering, and we may get angry.

Every sense organ has its corresponding sense object.

- For example, the sense organ of the eye has the visual objects.
- The sense organ of the ear has the sense object of sound.
- Each sense organ, when interacting with the sense objects, has the power to elicit various emotions in us.

Buddhists don't wish to manipulate atoms for some ordinary worldly incentive, such as seeking monetary gain.

- The main purpose of studying the material world through Buddhism is to learn how to overcome the causes and conditions of destructive emotions.

There are some schools of Buddhism, like the materialists, the realist philosophers, who conduct a rigorous study of phenomena.

- Their main purpose is to overcome all of the afflictive emotions.

- For this reason they practice meditation.

When we speak of this aspect of mindfulness called "mindfulness of the body" it includes:

- Not only our own physical bodies but also all other physical bodies and the material world.

Intellectual study of phenomena cannot free us from destructive emotions.

- To overcome all the emotions, we have to look deeper and deeper through meditation.
- Mindfulness gives us insight into the material components of our bodies as well as into the outside material world.
- This insight also extends well beyond the scope of what is apparent.

Apparent things are objects perceived through our first five sense organs.

- The insight we gain through mindfulness is more profound and has more to do with the sixth sense organ of mental consciousness.

Insight is gained through a meditative state of mind.

- In Buddhism this is considered a sixth sense organ, which is known as the mind or mental consciousness.

- When that mind is sharpened through meditation, and our insight grows deeper and deeper, we may see something which we have never seen before.

Ordinarily our perceptions remain at a very gross level.

- Through mindfulness, we are able to see something which is far more subtle.
- With this meditative insight, all material objects are recognized as part of the mindfulness of body.

As our insight becomes more refined, we see a greater truth or reality.

- Reality will appear very different from how we had previously seen the phenomenal world.

There is a big difference between how we see a material object, and how the Noble Ones, the enlightened masters, see the same object.

- The enlightened ones see the purity in all things.
- They have reached the third level of seeing, which is the level of pure vision.

Without that pure vision, what we see in the world is based on our karma.

- How we perceive the outer world is actually entirely based on our inner conditions.

- For example, when we see something visually alluring, some color or shape we are attracted to, that beauty is not necessarily inherent to that object.

- As the saying goes, "Beauty lies in the eye of the beholder."

In Buddhist understanding, attraction and aversion are a result of our emotions and karma.

- This karma is based on our past habitual patterns.

- When something generates an agreeable condition within us, when we feel very drawn to something, it is considered a "karmic link."

- Based on our past experiences, we have developed an affinity for certain objects or places or people.

All of these experiences of outer objects are based on what yogis call the "karmic vision."

- These perceptions are all based on our individual karma.

- That's why what we experience is not a universal truth.

For example, while humans can see a certain color or shape, cats and dogs may have a very different relationship to these same visual objects.

- Even among humans, our perception of each object, and our resulting emotions, are as individual as our respective karmas.

How we perceive reality, at our level, is based entirely on our inner conditions.

- That's why it's called "karmic vision."
- Karmic visions are personal as well as collective.

When we speak of "collective karma," it refers to the fact that certain groups of beings perceive things in a similar way.

- For example, humans have certain shared visions of reality.
- But within humanity, each person still has his or her own personal karma, which is unique.

As humans, we experience some things in an agreeable way.

- Within such collectively agreeable experiences, we can still have personally disagreeable responses.
- This has more to do with our karma than with the object itself.

This is why Buddha said that these personal karmic experiences are all relative.

- These experiences are not independent or universal.
- We often try to project a collective karmic experience as being universally true.
- When we conduct a thorough investigation, however, it becomes clear that this is not the case.

We have to start from where we are.

- All the great Buddhist philosophers agree that we have to use the relative truth in order to see the ultimate truth.

Q & A

10 - 15 minutes: Lead the class through a short Q & A session.

Questions for Review:

- What are the four aspects of right effort?
- Into what three categories can the Four Noble Truths be placed?
- What training can right view and right intention be categorized under?
- What category applies to right mindfulness and concentration?
- How would you describe the first foundation of mindfulness— mindfulness of body?

Class Eighteen

The Four Foundations of Mindfulness Continued

Objectives

Students will learn:

- What is included in the mindfulness of feelings
- How consciousness arises in the mind
- How the fourth foundation of mindfulness gives insight into additional types of mental action

Class Outline

Introduction

5 minutes: Begin with a short 5 minute Shamatha meditation.

Lecture

60 minutes

Q & A

10 - 15 minutes: Lead the class through a short Q & A session.

Through meditative experience, we have to go deeper and deeper into our exploration of the nature of reality.

- Are all our material experiences now only relative truths?

- If so, then what is the ultimate truth?
- These are the questions that yogis are trying to answer through meditation.

Mindfulness of the body includes mindfulness of all material things.

- As long as we are in the desire realm or in the form realm, we will remain in a physical body.
- We have to use our personal experiences of our own physical bodies to understand outer phenomena.
- Since all material objects are composed of these same elemental atoms, we can know outer objects through mindfulness of our own bodies.

The only difference between us and the outer inanimate objects is that we are psychosomatic beings, operating from this interaction of mind and body.

- It is only consciousness that separates all sentient beings from other physical matter.
- As sentient beings, we are capable of awareness which leads us to exploration.

The mind and body also create great obstacles.

- When we possess all these emotions and karmic propensities, everything becomes a very complex puzzle.

- In order to better understand this, Buddha taught about the five aggregates, the twelve ayatanas (bases), and the eighteen dhatus (elements).
- He taught these aspects in order for us to look deeper and deeper into the nature of things.
- Mindfulness of the body allows us to examine the nature of the material world.

The second foundation of mindfulness is mindfulness of feelings, which corresponds with the second aggregate of feeling.

- Feelings are experienced through the mind and body.

Buddha taught that there are five different kinds of feelings.

- There are physical feelings of pain and pleasure, mental feelings of happiness and unhappiness, and neutral feelings.
- Neutral feelings can be physical, mental, or both.

Feeling is one of the most important aspects of our lives and personalities.

- Feeling plays such a big role in our experience because it is based directly on our egos and on our sense of self.
- Most of the things we do in our lives are motivated by our wish to feel more pleasure and happiness and to avoid pain and suffering.

- Most of the major decisions we make in our lives are based on our feelings rather than our intellects.

When we practice mindfulness of feelings, we examine where a sensation and/or a feeling is coming from.

- Through meditative insight we question the nature and properties of that feeling.
- Mindfulness of feeling allows us to know the basis of a particular reaction.

We treasure and cherish feelings of pleasure and happiness.

- As a result we get very attached to these rewarding experiences.
- This drives us to try harder and harder to attain more of these positive feelings.

Feeling is crucial to our human experience.

- As a result of our attachment to ourselves, we are easily subject to having hurt feelings.
- The minute someone says or does something that threatens our egos, we respond with pain or sadness or anger.

Everything we do in our lives is based on our desire for happiness and pleasure.

- The whole entertainment industry is built on our wish to feel good and on our need to be distracted from ourselves and our uncomfortable feelings.
- We find pleasure in watching movies about other people's emotional dramas.
- It allows us to forget ourselves and to feel less alone in our human experience.

Through meditative insight, we can come to see the true nature of our feelings.

- We can understand the source of these feelings and the ways in which they impact our reality.
- This is the second foundation— mindfulness of feeling.

The third foundation of mindfulness is mindfulness of mind and mental consciousness.

- This corresponds with the fifth aggregate Buddha taught, which is the aggregate of consciousness.

Consciousness arises in the mind.

- Each of the six sense organs have corresponding sense objects, which we have described.
- For example, the sense organ of the eye has the sense object of visual objects etc.

Each of these six sense objects also has a corresponding sense consciousness.

- When we see, when we hear, when we taste, when we experience any of the six sense objects, basic consciousness arises in the mind.

For example, when we see a visual object, then our mind arises as eye consciousness.

- Eye consciousness is the part of the mind that becomes present when a healthy eye organ and a visual object come together.

It takes all three of these factors: the eye organ, the visual object, and the eye consciousness for visual perception to arise in the present moment.

- If one of these three factors is missing, then we will not be able to see.

Buddha taught that these six consciousnesses are present.

- Just because they are present doesn't mean that they are not still based on emotions and defilements.

Although we perceive these apparent objects with our present consciousness, our projections are still based on the inner conditions of the basic mind.

- This basic mind is always traveling with us from moment to moment, from life to life.
- Basic mind is filled with emotions and karma which then determine how these sense organs experience the world around us.

This third foundation, mindfulness of the mind or mental consciousness, helps us see the true nature of these six sense consciousnesses.

- Where do they come from?
- Are they present all the time?
- What are their properties?
- Through meditation we will begin to see the nature of consciousness more clearly.

The fourth foundation of mindfulness is called mindfulness of dharma.

- Here dharma does not have the usual meaning of Buddhist teachings.
- In this context dharma means all phenomena.

This fourth foundation corresponds with the aggregates of ideation and formation.

- That fourth aggregate of formation is very complex and includes the entire Buddhist understanding of psychology.
- This is outlined thoroughly in the texts of the Abhidharma.

The aggregates of ideation and formation are included in the fourth foundation, mindfulness of dharma.

- As long as we have all these thoughts inside our minds, we create karma.
- Karma is the origin of all our experiences in our lives.
- As we have discussed, our entire experience of reality is based on our individual and collective karmic vision.
- As long as we have karmic vision, then nothing is universal.
- We are not seeing any ultimate truth. Our vision is relative.

Mindfulness of dharma does *not* include the first three foundations(mindfulness of body, feelings, and mind), but everything else we experience is included in this fourth foundation.

- Here we find insight into Buddhist psychology and into all the different kinds of mental actions.

When I say "psychology," I am referring to all the root positive and negative emotions and to all our mental activities.

- We usually say that desire, anger, and ignorance are the three fundamental destructive emotions.
- The fourth foundation, mindfulness of dharma, includes all the destructive emotions, as well as all the positive emotions like faith, concentration, and memory.

- Mindfulness of dharma also includes all the neutral emotions.

Our minds are constantly filled with mental activities.

- Our mental actions respond to what occurs circumstantially to our interactions with an apparent object.
- At any given moment, anger, jealousy, or attachment might take over the mind based on some internal or external event.

Whenever the mind interacts with an object, through the sense organs or through mental projections, a strong emotion is activated.

- Although we may feel that the whole mind is suddenly experiencing anger, we must remember that the other sleeping emotions are still existing in us.
- We may think that when we have strong anger we do not have any love. But love is still there inside us as a sleeping emotion.
- We tend to only focus on the emotions that are actively present.

All of the conflicting emotions are existing in our minds, but whenever one emotion overtakes all the others, we forget the sleeping emotions.

- We also forget the true nature of the mind.

The higher tantric teachings reveal that all the destructive emotions, by nature, are actually wisdom.

- In tantra we have all these wrathful deities, and we say they are arising out of wisdom.
- This profound practice is based on an understanding of this basic composition of our minds.

Mindfulness of dharma is the most complex of the four foundations and includes more of the aggregates. To review:

- The first foundation of mindfulness, mindfulness of body, relates only to the first aggregate of matter/form.
- The second foundation, mindfulness of feeling, relates only to the second aggregate of feeling/sensation.
- The third foundation, mindfulness of mind, relates solely to the fifth aggregate of mind/mental consciousness.
- The fourth foundation, mindfulness of dharma, relates to both the third and fourth aggregates of ideation and formation.
- Mindfulness of dharma is the most complex and includes all of a person's mental activities, emotions, and psychology.

Q & A

10 - 15 minutes: Lead the class through a short Q & A session.

Questions for Review:

- What is the second foundation of mindfulness?
- How would you describe "mindfulness of feeling"?
- What are the five types of feelings?
- How would you describe "mindfulness of mind?"
- What aggregates are included in "mindfulness of dharma"?

Class Nineteen

Further Insights on the Four Foundations

Objectives

Students will learn:

- The Four Insights: impermanence, suffering, insubstantiality, and emptiness
- How the Four Foundations of Mindfulness help us gain a deeper understanding of these Four Insights
- The reasons why Buddha taught the First Noble Truth of Suffering and the Second Noble Truth of the Origin of Suffering
- The role of the ego in increasing our suffering
- A deeper understanding of insubstantiality and impermanence

Class Outline

Introduction

5 minutes: Begin with a short 5 minute Shamatha meditation.

Lecture

60 minutes

Q & A

10 minutes: Lead the class through a short Q & A session.

Insight into Impermanence

When we investigate our experience through these Four Foundations of Mindfulness:

- We see the nature of outside objects as well as the nature of our internal projection of objects.
- We attempt to integrate this in order to overcome the ego and to gain a more noble understanding.

The more we examine these four foundations of mindfulness, the more we realize that they are all impermanent.

- Our physical bodies and matter are impermanent.
- Our feelings, our consciousness, and all of the core emotions are impermanent. They are changing every moment.

When we see something beautiful, or when we feel something pleasurable, it brings us happiness, and we get attached to those objects or that experience.

- When we grow attached to an object or an experience, we try to make it permanent.
- This creates so much conflict and unhappiness because it is impossible to make that experience last.

Only through meditation will we learn to see the true nature of things.

- The more we meditate, the more we will see that every moment our physical bodies are changing.
- Every moment our feelings are changing.
- Every moment our minds are changing.
- Every moment our emotions are changing.

As a result we come to accept impermanence.

- Impermanence is the opposite of our wishes and our desires.
- We all want to have a permanently healthy body. When our bodies begin to age and to decay, they become a great source of mental and physical pain.

The suffering we experience as a result of physical pain is based largely on our egos.

- Our egos believe that our bodies should be young and beautiful forever.
- Our egos strongly resist the conditioned nature of things.

We believe that having these wonderful young bodies and all these fresh material things will bring us more pleasure.

- The truth is that even when these things bring us happiness in our youth, they are sowing seeds of future suffering.
- Inevitably we will lose these strong agile bodies and these wonderful possessions, and that loss will bring us pain.

Insight into Suffering

As long as we have feelings, they are based on ego.

- And as long as anything is based on ego, it is based on the root destructive emotions.
- Due to this fact, then even pleasure and happiness are also part of our destructive emotions.

Eventually we will come to see that all feelings and pleasures based on our bodies and sensations, or based on ideas and emotions, are actually a form of suffering.

- The more deeply we look, the more we will recognize the reality of the Second Noble Truth, the origin of suffering.
- Whatever is impermanent, changing, and aging is creating suffering.

The origin of suffering is very hard to accept because it goes against the wishes of our egos.

- Our egos are wishing for pleasure and happiness all the time.
- Our natural condition of suffering is the opposite of how we want to feel.

If we return to our early discussion of the First Noble Truth, we see that Buddha taught that suffering includes all feelings.

- This includes even pleasurable and neutral feelings.

- This is because all feelings are based on the destructive emotions of the ego.

Buddha didn't teach the Noble Truth of suffering and mindfulness of suffering in order to make us more miserable!

- Students sometimes ask me, "We already have so much pain and suffering in our lives, why does Buddha have to tell us that even our pleasure is suffering?"
- The reason that Buddha taught this was to help us achieve complete freedom from suffering.

In order to achieve this we have to be realistic and pragmatic.

- Insight related with suffering is critical to understanding the path to freedom.

Insight into Insubstantiality

When we delve deeper, we come to see that everything is insubstantial. Even physicists and psychologists are reaching the same conclusions:

- We cannot find any permanence in our emotions.
- There is no inherent existence of even a subatomic particle.
- There is no permanent basis for matter, feelings, ideas, and all phenomena.

Insight into Emptiness

The fourth insight is that not only are these things insubstantial, but their very nature is emptiness.

- Matter is empty.
- Feeling is empty.
- Mind is empty.
- All of the emotions are empty.

Those who are enlightened and who have achieved nirvāṇa realize this empty nature through the mindfulness of these Four Foundations.

- That is how they achieve enlightenment. Then they are finally free from all pain and suffering.

The more we investigate, the more there is to see.

- From impermanence we see emptiness. From emptiness we see the ultimate truth or ultimate nature.

This realization is the purpose of The Four Foundations of Mindfulness.

- These four foundations are taught primarily in the Hinayana Buddhist tradition.
- This is the main practice within countries such as Burma, Thailand, and Sri Lanka.

In the Mahayana tradition, in texts like "The Heart Sutra," we learn that, "Form is emptiness, emptiness is form; form is no other than emptiness, emptiness is no other than form."

- In the Vajrayana Buddhist tradition we have very profound sadhana meditation practices, which provide deep insight into this emptiness-nature.

All of these Buddhist traditions are complimentary.

- The purpose of The Four Foundations of Mindfulness is to reveal the emptiness-nature of all of our five aggregates.
- When we see that form, feeling, ideation, formation, and consciousness are all empty by nature, then we have the realization of selflessness.

For the first time we see the true nature of our egos, which is egolessness.

- We see the true nature of the self, which is selflessness. At this point we begin to free ourselves from ignorance.

When we're free from ignorance, we're free from attachment and aversion.

- At that point we no longer create any karma.
- We experience the whole universe, including our personal experiences, as pure vision.

As long as we have egos, we will continue to have karmic experiences.

- The seventh branch of the Noble Eightfold Path— Right Mindfulness is based on these Four Foundations of Mindfulness and the four insights this mindfulness can produce.
- Right Mindfulness will ultimately lead us to pure vision and to the ultimate truth of selflessness.
- This is the purpose of all insight meditation.

Q & A

10 - 15 minutes: Lead the class through a short Q & A session.

Questions for Review:

- Why did the Buddha teach that all feeling is a form of suffering?
- What are some of the advantages of accepting impermanence?
- What does it mean to say that things are "insubstantial"?
- Why is it important to see emptiness?
- How does insight into emptiness help us to go beyond suffering?

Class Twenty

The Noble Eightfold Path: Right Concentration

Objectives

Students will learn:

- The detriments of mental distractibility
- How mental distraction impacts our lives
- The four objects of attachment

Class Outline

Introduction

5 minutes: Begin with a short 5 minute Shamatha meditation.

Lecture

60 minutes

Q & A

10 minutes: Lead the class through a short Q & A session.

The eighth and final branch of the Noble Eightfold Path is "Right Concentration."

- As we know, the main obstacle to good meditation is distraction.

- The more distracting our lives become, the more difficult it is to focus our attention.
- Not only are we missing these important elements of attention and concentration, but distraction also brings more negativities into our lives.

If we investigate the sources of these constant distractions, we will see that they are all rooted in the destructive emotions.

- The more ignorance we have, the more anger and attachment we have in our mental streams, the less attention we will have.

This constant state of distractibility produces more negative karma.

- Without attention, we are much less aware of our physical actions, our speech, and our thoughts.
- When we act without true awareness, we are creating causes and conditions for future suffering.

At a worldly level, this constant mental distraction also prevents us from performing well at our jobs.

- It interferes with our ability to communicate well with the people around us and to achieve success because we simply cannot focus our attention on the task in front of us.

- Instead we are always daydreaming. We are thinking about the past or the future.

- We are wondering what we'll eat for lunch or wishing we were doing something else.

- Often we are obsessing about something someone said that hurt our feelings.

Mental distraction impacts all facets of our lives.

- If you are a student, and your mind is constantly wandering, it can be extremely challenging to study properly or to write a term paper.

- If you are working at a stressful job, then your inability to concentrate on the task at hand can impact your performance.

- If you are in a relationship, and you cannot be present to your children or to your partner because you are always thinking about other things, then you will experience conflict and disappointment within your family.

If we look closely in this way, we see that distraction is not just an issue when it comes time to meditate.

- Distraction is actually impacting our lives on every level, and meditation is the first step in beginning to examine those habitual patterns.

Unless we begin to break down those habitual patterns through meditation while we are alive, then even when we die that distracted mind will continue.

- After death, we will experience the bardo stage as a series of rushing distracted dreams, and we will take rebirth with that same disoriented mind.

When the mind is plagued with distractions, it is said to resemble a waterfall.

- All the emotions and all the karma come rushing over us, pushing us further and further down, producing more and more negativities.

The main cause of distraction is our unexamined destructive emotions.

- This is especially true for us humans living here in the desire realm.
- This realm is filled with craving and attachment. We are driven by our need for desirable objects to consume.

Out of all of these objects of attachment, our strongest desire is for other humans.

- Our other greatest attachment is towards the objects which we wish to possess.
- Our need for human relationships and our desire to have many possessions are driving forces in our lives.

The most direct method to overcome distraction is through meditation.

- At the highest level of meditation we reach this state of concentration or "samadhi."

There are four different levels of concentration in the form realm and four levels in the formless realm.

- These eight levels are all considered worldly concentrations.

These meditations in the form and formless realms can help us calm our emotions and achieve deep peace.

- But these worldly concentrations don't necessarily help us transcend all three realms of samsara to achieve complete liberation.

In the Theravada/Hinayana tradition of meditation, the aim of meditation practice is to achieve nirvāna and to go beyond samsara entirely.

- The method of practice in the Theravadan tradition is based entirely on renunciation.
- Renunciation means seeing that the nature of our lives is pain and suffering.
- Due to this realization we then wish to renounce the whole cycle of suffering and to achieve the cessation, the nirvāna.

Shamatha Meditation

Based on this renunciation, we then practice shamatha meditation.

- Shamatha is also known as "calm-abiding" meditation.

According to the texts of the Abhidharma, there are two methods for practicing shamatha meditation.

- The first method is to use shamatha practice as an antidote to desire.
- Since we live in the desire realm, desire is the strongest destructive emotion for us humans.
- In order to overcome this strong, active desire and attachment, we need to know why we have these emotions.

The Four Objects of Attachment

Shamatha meditation can help us to overcome the four objects of attachment.

- These objects are: color, shape, touch, and attention.

Our desire for visual objects is especially strong.

- We are drawn to objects because of their color, shape, design, and all of their appealing visual characteristics.

Our sense of touch is also a strong source of attachment.

- We want something to feel good to us.

- Whether it is the touch of another person, the feel of something soft under our hands, or even the feel of warm sunlight on our skin, touch is something we crave.
- Anything tangible that we find pleasurable can become a source of attachment.

The fourth object of attachment is attention. We crave the attention of others.

- We crave recognition and appreciation and love.
- We want to do well in our lives and achieve some level of success.

Shamatha meditation can help us to overcome these four objects of attachment by giving us antidotes.

- In order to overcome our attachment to color, we have to do shamatha practice based on undesirable color.
- In order to overcome our desire for shape we have to do shamatha meditation on an undesirable shape.

For example, if we are attached to the beautiful body of someone we desire, then we can meditate on that shape becoming very unattractive.

- If we are attached to the feel of something being smooth or soft, then we have to do shamatha meditation on an undesirable texture.

- If we are attached to recognition, then we can meditate on the negative side effects of that attention.

Shamatha Meditation on a Corpse or Skeleton

- Meditation on a human corpse is a very effective method for counteracting these objects of attachment.
- The Abhidharma texts describe nine meditations on a corpse to work through these four different attachments.

Buddha said that if we cannot meditate on the specific color or shape of the corpse, if that is too gruesome or challenging at first, then we can also just meditate on the skeleton.

- The skeleton has the antidotal power to overcome all of the four objects of attachment.
- Through our practice we try to overcome the active desire and attachment so that our shamatha meditation will be effective.

Q & A

10 - 15 minutes: Lead the class through a short Q & A session.

Questions for Review:

- What is the main obstacle to a good meditation?
- What lies at the root of our distraction?

- What are some of the ways in which we are impacted by distraction?
- What does the term "Shamatha" mean?
- What are the four objects of attachment?

Class Twenty-One

Right Concentration Continued

Objectives

Students will learn:

- How to use Shamatha practice to calm a distracted mind
- Six different ways to conduct meditation on the breath
- How to practice insight meditation on the four foundations of mindfulness

Class Outline

Introduction

5 minutes: Begin with a short 5 minute Shamatha meditation.

Lecture

60 minutes

Q & A

10 minutes: Lead the class through a short Q & A session.

Shamatha Meditation on the Breath

The second method of shamatha meditation is designed for those people who have lots of concepts, lots of thoughts, lots of inner chattering all the time.

- This inner chatter is not necessarily related to attachment and desire. It can include anger, neutral thoughts, and all the intellectual distractions.
- When the mind is very busy in this way, it is very good to do shamatha meditation focused on the breath.

The Abhidharma texts describe six different ways to use the breathing as an object of meditation.

The first breathing meditation is called "counting."

- You can count to ten over and over again.
- Beginning on the inhalation you count "one," and on the exhalation you count "two."
- Each time you get distracted you return again to the beginning.

It is emphasized that you should not count higher than ten, or it could make you more active and distracted.

- It is also advised that you don't count fewer than ten, or you may become lazy in your practice.

The second breathing meditation is called "following."

- In this exercise you follow the movement of the inhalation, the circulation of the air inside you, and then the exhalation.

- In this way, you try to follow the movement of the air in your body.

The third breathing meditation is called "placing." With "placing" you pay complete attention to the movement of the breath in your body.

- With concentration you focus on the circulation of the breath from the nostrils down to the feet and back up again, like a rope of air.

When you concentrate in this manner, you see that the air is continuously circulating.

- You can notice the temperature of the air.

- When you can focus your concentration on the whole circulation of the air simultaneously, then that is the third shamatha practice called "placing."

The fourth practice is called "more placing."

- By observing the movement of the air inside you, you begin to have the realization that air is not just composed of the air element.

- As your shamatha practice strengthens, you begin to experience that air contains all four elements.

- You also begin to realize that air is supporting the mind and the emotions.
- Through this practice you begin to see that air is involved in all of the five aggregates— form, feeling, ideation, formation and consciousness.
- This fourth practice of "more placing" deepens your concentration on the breath.

The fifth practice is called "modification."
- With modification, you use whatever concentration you have achieved based on the air meditations to increase the cultivation of spirituality inside of you.
- This in turn allows you to achieve higher and higher levels of realization.
- The concentration is applied in order to increase the positive spiritual qualities and then decrease the negative destructive emotions.

The sixth practice is called "complete purification."
- You use that "modification" practice to continue cultivating the positive spiritual qualities and to completely purify all the destructive emotions and negativities.
- Eventually this cultivation will help you to go beyond all the negative emotions and negative karma.

We can choose the object of our shamatha meditation depending on our temperaments.

- If we have lots of clinging and desire, we can do shamatha meditation on the corpse or skeleton.

- If we are filled with many ideas and concepts, we can quiet the mind by doing the shamatha meditation on the breath.

Both of these objects of meditation include the nine stages of shamatha.

- The first three stages of shamatha are to overcome the distractions so you can pay attention to the object.

- The next three stages are to strengthen that attention.

- The last three stages of shamatha use the attention you have achieved and apply it to the result, which is concentration.

After achieving some experience with shamatha meditation, you can proceed to the next meditation which is mindfulness practice or insight meditation.

- Mindfulness practice is based on the seventh branch of the Noble Eightfold path.

- Only when you have good shamatha practice and concentration will you be able to use that attention to achieve the insight meditation.

For insight meditation, you start with the Four Foundations of Mindfulness, which we have discussed in an earlier class.

- Through cultivating Mindfulness of the Body, you have the realization that the physical body is the base of all suffering, and that helps you to accept the First Noble Truth, the truth of suffering.

As a result of our physical bodies, we are subjected to all three kinds of suffering: suffering of suffering, suffering of change, and suffering of conditioned existence.

- Because we have a physical body, we experience the suffering of suffering, and we are unable to avoid sickness and pain.
- Because of our physical bodies, we also have the suffering of change since nothing pleasurable can last.
- Furthermore, as a result of our physical bodies, we will all be subjected to old age and death, and we will have to experience the suffering of conditioned existence.

Through practicing Mindfulness of the Body, we come to recognize that this physical body is the base of all three kinds of suffering.

- This leads us to a profound understanding of the First Noble Truth, the truth of suffering.

The second mindfulness practice is Mindfulness of Feelings.

- When we look more closely, we realize that feelings are the cause of all our craving.

- This craving creates all the causes and conditions for our afflictive emotions and suffering. By practicing Mindfulness of Feelings, we will come to the realization that feeling is the origin of all our suffering.

- This will deepen our understanding of the Second Noble Truth of the origin of suffering.

The third mindfulness practice is Mindfulness of the Mind.

- Through this practice, we come to the realization that the mind is impermanent, and the mind can cease.

- At the present moment, our minds are the basis for the self.

- Through the practice of Mindfulness of the Mind, we can develop insight into the Third Noble Truth of cessation.

The fourth mindfulness practice is Mindfulness of the Dharma, which in this context means phenomena. Through this practice we come to see that within the dharma there are things to abandon, and there are things to accept.

- Based on learning what to accept and what to reject, we will come to know the Fourth Noble Truth of the path.

Including the Four Foundations of Mindfulness, there are thirty-seven noble practices from the Hinayana tradition that instruct us on how to achieve the nirvāṇa.

- The Mahayana tradition takes this concentration to another level.

- After taking the Bodhisattva vow, we cultivate loving-kindness and compassion.

- In the Mahayana tradition we use the six paramitas, also known as the "six perfections" practice, to achieve complete enlightenment.

Q & A

10 - 15 minutes: Lead the class through a short Q & A session.

Questions for Review:

- How would you describe the first and second type of breath practice used in Shamatha meditation?

- In the third form of breath practice, what do you place your attention on?

- How does "more placing" differ from "placing?"

- What is the practice of modification? How does modification support complete purification?

- How does the object of shamatha practice differ from the object (or objects) of mindfulness practice?

Made in the USA
Middletown, DE
27 February 2017